Primate Utilization and Conservation

Primate Utilization and Conservation ⌐ 1975

Edited by

Gordon Bermant, Ph.D.
Coordinator, Behavioral and Social Sciences
Battelle Memorial Institute
Seattle, Washington
and
Affiliate Professor of Psychology
University of Washington
Seattle, Washington

and

Donald G. Lindburg, Ph.D.
Professor of Anthropology
Georgia State University
Atlanta, Georgia

*A volume based on a conference held at
Battelle Seattle Research Center,
Seattle, Washington, August 11–12, 1972*

A WILEY-INTERSCIENCE PUBLICATION

JOHN WILEY & SONS New York • London • Sydney • Toronto

Library of Congress Cataloging in Publication Data:

Main entry under title:
Primate utilization and conservation.

    Based on the New Concepts in Primate Production Conference held at Battelle Seattle Research Center, Seattle, Aug. 11-12, 1972.
    "A Wiley-Interscience publication."
    Includes bibliographies.
I. Bermant, Gordon, ed.   II. Lindburg, Donald G.,
2. Primates—Congresses.   3. Wildlife conservation—
Congresses.   4. Primate breeding—Congresses.
1. Bermant, Gordon, ed. II.   Lindburg, Donald G.,
1932-   ed. III. New Concepts in Primate Production
Conference, Battelle Seattle Research Center, 1972.

QL737.P9P675   619'.98   74-13570
ISBN 0-471-07070-X

Printed in the United States of America

10 9 8 7 6 5 4 3 2 1

Participants

New Concepts in Primate Production Conference

Gordon Bermant, Ph.D.
Coordinator, Behavioral and
Social Sciences
Battelle Memorial Institute
Seattle, Washington
Affiliate Professor of Psychology
University of Washington
Seattle, Washington

Francis C. Cadigan, Jr., M.D.
Director of Medical Research
Headquarters, U.S. Army Medical
Research and Development Command
Washington, D. C.

C. Ray Carpenter, Ph.D., D.Sc.
Senior Fellow
The East–West Center
Honolulu, Hawaii

Robert W. Cooper, Ph.D.
Biologist, Division de Parques
Nacionales y Vida Silvestre
INDERENA
Bogota, Colombia
Volunteer, Smithsonian-Peace Corps
Environmental Program
Colombia/Peace Corps
Conservation Program

W. Richard Dukelow, Ph.D.
Associate Professor and Director
Endocrine Research Unit
Michigan State University
East Lansing, Michigan

John Stephen Gartlan, Ph.D.
Helminthiasis Research Unit
Institut de Reshesches Medicales
Kumba, West Cameroon
United Republic of Cameroon

William J. Goodwin, Ph.D.
Director, Primate Research
Center Program
Animal Resources Branch
Division of Research Resources
National Institutes of Health
Bethesda, Maryland

Robert W. Goy, Ph.D.
Director, Wisconsin Regional Primate
Research Center
Professor, Department of Psychology
University of Wisconsin
Madison, Wisconsin

v

Barbara Harrisson, Ph.D.
Senior Research Associate
Department of Anthropology
Cornell University
Ithaca, New York

Andrew G. Hendrickx, Ph.D.
Research Physiologist
California Primate Research Center
University of California, Davis
Davis, California

Jorge Hernandez-Camacho, Ph.D.
Chief, Wildlife Subprogram
Division de Parques Nacionales y
Vida Silvestre
INDERENA
Bogota, Colombia

Keith R. Hobbs, Ph.D.
Medical Research Council Laboratories
Laboratory Animals Centre
Carshalton, Surrey, England

Robert L. Hummer, V.M.D., M.P.H.
Veterinary Consultant
The American Humane Association
San Antonio, Texas

Junichiro Itani, D.Sc.
Assistant Professor of
Physical Anthropology
Koyoto University
Sakyo, Kyoto, Japan

Kenneth T. Kirton, Ph.D.
Research Associate
The Upjohn Company
Kalamazoo, Michigan

Lim Boo Liat
Head, Division of Medical Ecology
Institute for Medical Research
Kuala Lumpur, Malaysia

Donald G. Lindburg, Ph.D.
Department of Anthropology
Georgia State University
Atlanta, Georgia

Col. Edwin D. McMeen
New England Regional Primate
Research Center
Southborough, Mass.

Akisato Nishimura, M.S.
Research Assistant,
Primate Research Institute
Kyoto University
Inuyama, Aichi, Japan

Michael A. Nolan, President
Primate Imports Corporation
Port Washington, New York

Amos E. Palmer, D.V.M.
Research Veterinarian
Infectious Diseases Branch, D&FR
National Institute of Neurological
Disease and Stroke
National Institutes of Health
Bethesda, Maryland

Charles H. Phoenix, Ph.D.
Assistant Director, ORPRC
Head, Primate Behavior Section
Oregon Regional Primate
Research Center
Beaverton, Oregon

M. S. Rai, President
PrimeLabs, Incorporated
Farmington, New Jersey

Thelma Rowell, Ph.D.
Adjunct Professor
Department of Zoology
University of California
Berkeley, California

M. Farooq Siddiqi, Ph.D.
Department of Geography
Aligarh Muslim University
Aligarh, India

M. Rafiq Siddiqi, Ph.D.
Commonwealth Bureau of Helminthology
St. Albans, Hertfordshire
England

Anita Schwaier, Ph.D.
Department of Toxicology
Battelle-Institute e.V.
Frankfurt/Main
Germany

Charles H. Southwick, Ph.D.
Professor of Pathobiology
The Johns Hopkins University
School of Hygiene and Public Health
Baltimore, Maryland

Orville A. Smith, Ph.D.
Director
Regional Primate Research Center
University of Washington
Seattle, Washington

Richard W. Thorington, Jr., Ph.D.
Associate Curator of Mammals
Department of Vert. Zool.
Smithsonian Institution
Washington, D.C.

Michael J. Welcroft, D.V.M., V.S.
Assistant Director and Head
Animal Resources Department
Connaught Laboratories Limited
Willowdale
Ontario, Canada

Robert A. Whitney, Jr., D.V.M.
Chief
Veterinary Resources Branch
Division of Research Services
National Institutes of Health
Bethesda, Maryland

Martin D. Young, Director
Gorgas Memorial Laboratory
Balboa Heights, Canal Zone

Preface

A concern with the interactions of biomedical research needs with the future of nonhuman primates in natural settings lay behind the decision of the Battelle Memorial Institute to sponsor a conference titled "New Concepts in Primate Production" at Battelle's Seattle Research Center on August 11–12, 1972. All funds were provided by the Behavioral and Social Science Program of Battelle Institute, which is a division of Battelle that sponsors worthwhile research and conferences philanthropically. Coordinator of Battelle Institute activities at the time was Dr. R. W. Dayton.

In 1970 Gordon Bermant and Sripati Chandrasekhar, Center Fellow and Visiting Fellow, respectively, at the Battelle Seattle Research Center, wrote a brief letter to *Science* in favorable response to the article on Indian monkey demography and prospects by Southwick, Siddiqi and Siddiqi.* Among the respondents to the letter was Donald G. Lindburg, who suggested that the ideas sketched by Bermant and Chandrasekhar and those held by himself were sufficiently overlapping to warrant further discussion. As discussion progressed, the idea of a small working conference emerged as a sound way to try to further understanding and action toward practical solution of the problems faced by the animals and those of us who need them to pursue research. It was never imagined that the Battelle meeting was the first of its sort, nor by any means the largest. The intent was to limit the participation to less than 35 individuals representing relevant interest groups, on the hope that more intense interaction would be promoted by the relatively small number of participants. The organizers were fortunate to have the counsel of Dr. Wil-

*We are pleased to reprint this excellent paper as Chapter 11 of the current volume. It is the only chapter not presented at the original conference.

liam J. Goodwin of the National Institutes of Health and Dr. Orville A. Smith of the University of Washington during the planning phase.

The papers invited for presentation were grouped in three categories: current research needs and estimates of future trends, problems existing at sources of current supply, and experiments in the production and ranching of primates and their maintenance under seminatural conditions. Additionally, at the conclusion of the meeting, all participants were asked to write down their views of the issues the papers and general discussions had made most salient to them. We have relied on these comments in the final chapter of the volume and in a summary of the meeting published elsewhere.*

The impact of a two-day meeting of a few dozen persons is usually difficult to ascertain. As organizers and editors, we are pleased to have been able to facilitate the publication of the important ideas and findings of our contributors. At least one immediately practical outcome of the meeting was the institution, shortly thereafter, of the "Primates Wanted and Available" notices in the weekly *Current Primate References* publication of the Primate Information Center, Regional Primate Research Center, University of Washington. Also particularly pleasing to us, although it is by no means a result of the conference, is the *addendum* to the chapter by J. S. Gartlan wherein he reports the successful establishment of two new preserves in the biologically and geologically important Cameroon–Congo Coastal Strip. This successful effort can serve as a model for other such ventures.

Finally, before turning to the work of the contributors directly, we should like to thank the entire staff of the Battelle Seattle Research Center for their thoroughly professional aid in arranging and conducting the meeting. In particular we are grateful to our Battelle editor, Ms. Ellen Brandt, from whose high standards and great tact we all benefited.

GORDON BERMANT

DONALD G. LINDBURG

Seattle, Washington
Atlanta, Georgia
May, 1974

**Bermant, G., and Lindburg, D.G. (1973). New concepts in primate production. *Journal of Medical Primatology*, 2:324-340). We are grateful to Dr. J. Moor-Jankowski of the *Journal* for his invitation to publish this rather extensive summary of the meeting.

Contents

Tables

Primate Utilization and Conservation

CHAPTER 1

Gordon Bermant
Donald G. Lindburg

INTRODUCTION
AND OVERVIEW

This book and the conference proceedings on which it is based are the results of continuing concern by the biomedical research community for the future of naturally occurring nonhuman primate populations and the development of enlarged domestic primate production programs. These two issues, conservation and production of nonhuman primates, are together one example of the set of problems that arises at the interface of activities between more and less industrialized nations. The former are the customers, the latter the suppliers of nonhuman primates. The needs of the biomedical community, while quantitatively variable as a function of available research financing, are nevertheless almost completely dependent on continued availability of animals in the native environments: more than 90 percent of the nonhuman primates used for research in the United States are imported. Hence the research community has a pressing interest in the continuing viability of natural populations. Many researchers are also sensitive to the esthetics of conservation, hence they worry about the high probability that a number of primate species are endangered by extinction in the near future.

The scientists and officials of countries that supply nonhuman primates may also be sensitive to these issues and just as concerned for the continued integrity of local fauna. But they are faced daily with the realities of modernization: increases in lumbering, mining, and agriculture, as well as burgeoning population growth. Coupled to these vectors of social change is the continuation of practices against nonhuman primates that no longer seem harmless. The zoo and pet trades and the use of monkeys and apes for food are examples of traditional activities that have combined with the effects of modernization to place enormous, perhaps fatal, pressures on a number of primate species. But the governments of primate-producing countries cannot very well afford to place the interests of their nonhuman species ahead of the important interests of the human population. Moreover, these governments may legitimately take offense at suggestions from enormously affluent Americans that they ought to spend more time and money caring for their monkeys and apes at a time when their peoples are awake to the realities of the discrepant living standards between themselves and ourselves and to the hope that the differences may be reduced through industrial modernization. Only in nations that have traditionally scrupled against destruction of some non-human primate species (India, Japan) are there cultural mechanics for conservation that will not· be perceived as meddlesome interventions. When men and monkeys engage in a zero-sum game, the monkeys will surely lose.

All this is obvious enough. The basic question is what to do. Those who attempt to answer the question must first accept that conservationist or preservationist goals and biomedical research needs are by no means identical. While some researchers are also conservationists, and while some primate research fields (ethology in particular) are highly dependent on the maintenance of natural populations in historical habitats, a great bulk of biomedical research could be done effectively (ignoring dollar costs for the moment) with ranch- or laboratory-bred animals. Presently, of course, the independence of research from natural populations is only theoretical, because adequate breeding programs do not exist. However, given the assumption that the availability of at least some useful research species (e.g., *Aotus trivirgatus, Pan troglodytes*) will become increasingly problematic, there is good reason to begin to plan for breeding programs that will meet research needs by the time feral animals are no longer available. The best ways to achieve this objective are still much open to debate; several chapters in this volume address different alternatives. At this point in the discussion we want to emphasize only that plans for breeding programs should perhaps proceed with the working assumption that at the end of n years there will be no more feral animals. Planning done on this basis might lead to different technical decisions (for example, in regard to the degree of inbreeding allowable) than would be made on the assumption that feral animals could be brought into the breeding pool on a systematic basis.

One might hope, of course, that the development of breeding programs would reduce the pressures of research-related trapping on some natural populations sufficiently that the life expectancies of these populations would be increased. In fact it was an initial assumption on the part of the current authors, prior to our conference, that the number of animals trapped for research purposes constituted an appreciable proportion of the total lost by natural populations each year. It now appears to us, however, based on material presented here and subsequent findings, that the rate of loss of at least some natural populations used as pools for research animals would not change markedly even if research demands went to zero. Lumbering, mining, agriculture, hunting, and trapping for pet and zoo trades all take their tolls in numbers difficult to measure and impossible to regulate. The number of animals taken for research in a year is better known (e.g., approximately 85,000 for United States research in 1968, 60,000 in 1966 and 1970) and more easily controllable by both donor and accepter. Unfortunately, increasing the degree of regulation on scientific use alone would probably not produce a benefit for the natural population worth the increased costs of the regulation. This is particularly true from the fiscal perspective of the supplying countries, for which primate exports are an insignificant proportion of total export income (e.g., the data for Colombia as presented by Cooper and Hernandez-Camacho in this volume). This is not to say that researchers can be callous in their concern for natural populations, but rather that they are more in the position of a secondary victim than a primary villain in regard to the depletion of natural populations. It is enlightened biomedical self-interest rather than misdirected altruism that should motivate the rapid expansion of efforts to produce nonhuman primates of several species. This perspective coupled with intelligent, planned efforts at conservation and preservation (e.g., as described by Gartlan in this volume) seem to provide the best combination for effective action.

When one speaks of increased efforts to breed "several species" in captive or semicaptive conditions, one is then placed in the position of having to make some decisions about the selection of certain species rather than others. It seems to us that the research community needs a plan that specifies how these decisions are to be made. Several factors will clearly enter the decision-making process: current-use data, estimates of future needs, basic research on the usefulness of given species as models for particular diseases, relative ease of breeding in captivity, costs, continued availability in natural populations, and so on. The question becomes how several factors are to be weighted in the decision-making process. On the basis of many criteria, for example, there is good reason to emphasize the production of rhesus monkeys: they are currently the most used species, there is no reason to believe their popularity is decreasing, a backlog of normative data is available for a number of preparations, they breed relatively easily in captivity, and so on. And yet the plan has drawbacks: the monkeys are fairly large and difficult to handle, they are still in relatively ample and inexpensive natural supply, and so on. How ought the advantages and disadvantages be weighed in coming to a decision about the allocation of available resources? How much money should be put into rhesus breeding programs as opposed to other macaque breeding programs? What is the relative research importance of the macaques, in general, as compared to larger species (e.g., baboons, apes) on the one hand, and smaller, perhaps more delicate but quite useful species (e.g., *Aotus trivirgatus*) on the other hand? How much effort should go into the definition and development of a "standard laboratory monkey"? What is the likelihood that very small members of the family (e.g., *Tupaia*) could serve research functions now served by larger, more expensive animals? These questions and others like them need to be raised, debated, tested, and resolved as systematically as possible, with the participation of all the relevant interest groups.

Research runs on money as well as ideas; sooner or later the costs and financing methods of new programs will need to be considered. At the present time the relation between nonhuman primate supply and demand places the cost of a feral animal substantially below the cost of one produced under human control. It is safe to predict that this will not be the case indefinitely, probably even for the relatively abundant species. But there appears to be more to the economic aspects of the problem than this basic point. For example, what relations between commercial users (e.g., pharmaceutical companies) and noncommercial users (e.g., universities) should obtain in the support of domestic breeding programs? Should federal taxes spent through traditional channels (e.g., Primate Center programs) provide the impetus, or ought there to be joint industrial–government sponsorship? Should breeding programs be run under strict contract or encouraged to proliferate in the marketplace? Given the substantial start-up costs of breeding colonies, what kinds of guarantees for continued need can be given to groups that might be willing to risk venture capital for a fair return? These and related economic questions might seem premature at the instant, but their careful consideration in the basic planning stages can prevent waste of time and money when needs become more imminent.

CHAPTER 2

William J. Goodwin

PRIMATE RESOURCES– CURRENT STATUS AND FUTURE NEEDS

To answer some of the major questions in many biomedical areas of significance, it is evident that appropriate primate models are required for experimentation. During the past decade, we have witnessed a significant increase in research activities that employ primates as animal models as well as a considerable increase in the number of primates used. The research needs in the United States for both colony-bred and feral animals will undoubtedly increase in the future.

There is an ever-increasing concern on the part of many scientists regarding the availability of primates required for biomedical research investigations. This concern has been expressed on a number of occasions, but unfortunately little has been done to rectify the situation. Many of us concerned with primate research believe the primate supply problem has already reached a critical stage and that steps must be taken now to assure an adequate supply in the future.

There are several ways in which the use of primates in biomedical research has increased in recent years. The use of common primates such as the rhesus, squirrel monkey, baboon, and chimpanzee has increased in well-established research areas such as reproductive biology, behavior, and infectious diseases. These same species are also proving to be suitable animal models in many new areas of biomedical research including diabetes, atherosclerosis, immunology, organ transplantation, and numerous others. Certain other species possessing unique biological characteristics have been found to be invaluable for particular research purposes. A classic example is the use of the owl monkey in malaria chemotherapy research.

PRIMATE USE AND RESOURCES IN THE UNITED STATES

It is difficult to determine the total usage of primates in biomedical research in this country and even more difficult to anticipate the requirements for various species in the future. It may be useful, however, to review the overall trends in the use of various species during recent years and to identify the current population of primates in the major primate laboratories in this country.

The best information available on the numbers of primates used in research laboratories in the United States is that provided by the Institute of Laboratory Animal Resources in their annual laboratory animal surveys. A summary of the data obtained from these surveys for the period 1966 through 1970 is given in Table 1. As indicated in the table,

Table 1   *Trends in the Use of Primates in the United States (1966–1970)*[a]

Primate	1966	1967	1968	1969	1970
New World					
Cebidae	8,062	11,619	28,825	14,117	12,480
Callithrichidae	669	779	3,858	2,415	2,802
	8,731	12,398	32,683	16,532	15,282
Old World					
Cercopithecus spp.	7,522	7,200	5,262	5,852	3,017
Macaca mulatta	28,307	30,620	37,290	34,665	27,092
Macaca fascicularis	12,044	6,565	4,372	3,836	3,487
Macaca nemestrina	264	337	603	353	830
Macaca arctoides	557	679	1,174	486	863
Papio spp.	1,158	1,472	985	1,254	1,651
Pan spp.	253	383	378	302	221
	50,105	47,256	50,004	46,748	37,161
Miscellaneous	3,947	10,762	2,596	4,722	1,994
TOTAL	62,783	70,416	85,283	68,002	54,437[b]
Number of questionnaires returned	1,442	1,366	1,493	2,258	1,523
Percent returned	61	53	63	69	49

[a] Data obtained from ILAR surveys.

[b] Note that only 49 percent of the questionnaires were returned for 1970, making this data point less significant.

the total numbers of primates used increased rapidly until 1968, due to the increasing recognition of their importance in research and to the increase in federal biomedical research funds. The subsequent decrease, since 1969, is probably due to the decrease in available research funds and better utilization of primates by investigators.

Information on the research areas and the principal primate species utilized by a number of major primate laboratories in the United States has recently been gathered by the author. The National Institutes of Health have established and provided funding for seven Primate Research Centers in the United States (see Table 2). These centers conduct major programs in reproductive physiology, cardiovascular physiology, environmental health, infectious diseases, metabolic diseases, and neural and behavioral sciences and currently maintain a total of 7249 primates representing 32 species, as shown in Table 3.

Information on a number of other major primate laboratories is given in Tables 4–6. A total of approximately 22,860 primates are being used by these three types of laboratories in a variety of research areas includ-

Table 2   Primate Research Centers

Center and Location	Host University	Research Missions
Oregon PRC Beaverton, Oregon	University of Oregon	Reproductive biology Metabolic diseases Immune diseases
Delta PRC Covington, Louisiana	Tulane University	Infectious diseases Nutritional diseases
Yerkes PRC Atlanta, Georgia	Emory University	Neural and behavioral research Neoplastic and degenerative diseases
Washington PRC Seattle, Washington	University of Washington	Cardiovascular physiology Collaborative program
Wisconsin PRC Madison, Wisconsin	University of Wisconsin	Reproductive biology Neural and behavioral research
New England PRC Southborough, Massachusetts	Harvard University	Infectious diseases Collaborative program
California PRC Davis, California	University of California, Davis	Respiratory diseases Environmental toxicology

Table 3   Distribution of Nonhuman Primate Species in the Seven Primate Research Center (December 31, 1971)[a]

Primate Species	Number in Centers
Prosimii	
Tupaiidae	
Tupaia glis	50
Lemuridae	
Lemur catta	40
Lemur m. fulvus	52
Lemur macaco	13
Lemur mongoz	11
Lorisidae	
Galago crassicaudatus	100
Nycticebus coucang	24
Anthropoidea	
Callithrichidae	
Cebuella pygmaea	13
Saguinus oedipus	46
Cebidae	
Cebus albifrons	83
Cebus apella	373
Aotus trivirgatus	79
Callicebus moloch	32
Cercopithecidae	
Cercopithecus aethiops	102
Cercopithecus talapoin	52
Erythrocebus patas	90
Cercocebus atys	55
Papio anubis	139
Papio papio	92
Theropithecus gelada	21
Macaca mulatta	3,250
Macaca nemestrina	944
Macaca fascicularis	556
Macaca arctoides	281
Macaca radiata	212
Macaca cyclopis	125
Macaca fuscata	114
Macaca nigra	62
Presbytis entellus	38
Pongidae	
Pongo pygmaeus	36
Pan troglodytes	147
Gorilla gorilla	17
Total	7,249

[a] Only species where 10 or more animals are used are included here.

Table 4   Multidisciplinary Primate Laboratories in the United States (1972)

Laboratory	Research Areas	Primate Species Used
University Laboratories		
Caribbean Primate Research Center University of Puerto Rico San Juan, Puerto Rico	Behavior Reproductive biology	890 *M. mulatta*
Holloman Primate Facility Holloman Air Force Base New Mexico	Environmental toxicology	600 *M. mulatta* 95 *Pan troglodytes*
Laboratory Experimental Medicine and Surgery in Primates New York University Sterling Forest, New York	Immunology Reproductive biology Genetics	180 *Papio* spp. 100 *M. mulatta* 75 *Pan troglodytes*
Nonprofit Foundations Southwest Foundation for Research and Education San Antonio, Texas	Microbiology Endocrinology	619 *Papio* spp. 84 *Saguinus* spp. 40 *Pan troglodytes*
Gulf South Research Foundation New Iberia, Louisiana	Virology Toxicology	200 *M. Mulatta* 200 *S. sciureus*
Commercial Organizations Bionetics Research Laboratories, Inc. Kensington, Maryland	Virology Toxicology	2,100 *M. mulatta* 352 *M. fascicularis*
Hazleton Laboratories Inc. Falls Church, Virginia	Oncology Toxicology	525 *M. mulatta* 425 *M. fascicularis*

ing reproductive biology, infectious diseases, behavior, viral oncology, immunology, and dental research.

In addition to the increasing numbers of primates employed in research activities, it is interesting to note the growing number of research projects using primates. For example, the number of research projects in which primates were used in 1965 and in 1971, as reported by the Science Information Exchange, has increased from 666 to 1183. This is an increase of nearly 80 percent in spite of the decrease in federal research funds during the late 1960s. The number of documents in which primates were cited

Table 5   Specialized Primate Laboratories in the United States (1972)

Laboratory	Research Areas	Primate Species Used
Department of Physiology University of Pittsburgh Medical School Pittsburgh, Pennsylvania	Reproductive physiology	220 *M. mulatta*
Division of Reproductive Physiology University of Pennsylvania Medical School Philadelphia, Pennsylvania	Reproductive physiology	200 *M. mulatta*
Population Council Rockefeller University New York, New York	Reproductive biology	400 *M. mulatta*
Department of Laboratory Animal Medicine Bowman Gray Medical School Winston-Salem, North Carolina	Cardiovascular diseases	600 *S. sciureus*
Dental Sciences Institute University of Texas Houston, Texas	Dental research	400 *Saguinus* spp.
Department of Medicine and Microbiology Rush Presbyterian–St. Luke Medical Center Chicago, Illinois	Viral oncology	400 *Saguinus* spp.
Oak Ridge Associated University Oak Ridge, Tennessee	Immunology	500 *Saguinus* spp.

as having been used in research has also increased substantially. For example, the Primate Information Center of the Washington Primate Research Center listed some 5000 references in 1960, and by 1971 this number had increased to 35,000—a seven-fold increase in 11 years.

In considering the research needs for primates, one must also consider the selection of the proper species. Since there are some 80 genera and 240 species of primates, it is not likely that all these can or should be developed as laboratory models. The selection of certain desirable species for development has proven quite difficult. The use of several species has been well established; however, selection of these particular primates

Table 6   United States Government Primate Research Laboratories (1972)

Agency	Research Areas	Primate Species Used
National Institutes of Health Bethesda, Maryland	General biomedical	9,500 of many species
Center for Disease Control Atlanta, Georgia, and Phoenix, Arizona	Malaria Hepatitis	895 *Pan, Macaca, Saguinus, Aotus*
Environmental Protection Administration Perrine, Florida	Toxicology	320 *Macaca, Saimiri*
Walter Reed Army Institute of Research Washington, D.C.	Neural sciences Infectious diseases	865 *Macaca, Papio Aotus, Saimiri*
Medical Laboratory Edgewood Arsenal, Maryland	Toxicology Behavior	365 *Macaca, Saimiri*
Aerospace Medical Laboratory Wright-Patterson Air Force Base Ohio	Toxicology Preventive Medicine	265 *Macaca, Papio*
School of Aerospace Medicine Brooks Air Force Base, Texas	Physiology Radiobiology	1,330 *Macaca*
Naval Medical Institute Bethesda, Maryland	Immunology Dental research	150 *Macaca, Papio. Saimiri*
Naval Aerospace Medical Research Laboratory Pensacola, Florida	Behavior	95 *Macaca, Saimiri*
Naval Biomedical Research Laboratory Oakland, California	Immunology Microbiology	90 *Macaca, Cercopithecus*
Armed Forces Institute of Pathology Washington, D.C.	Experimental surgery	80 *Macaca*

was probably based on their availability rather than on their biologic characteristics. Tables 3–6 indicate the species that are currently used extensively. These include *Macaca mulatta, Macaca fascicularis, Macaca nemestrina, Saimiri sciureus, Papio cynocephalus, Aotus trivirgatus, Saguinus nigricollis, Saguinus mystax,* and *Pan troglodytes.*

The scientific community in the United States must recognize that it cannot totally depend on the importation of primates for its future supply.

The encroachment of civilization on primate habitats in developing countries is rapidly reducing the numbers of primates available in the world. Unfortunately, some species have already been reduced to the point of extinction and can no longer be considered for research purposes. In addition, political and legal restrictions are being placed on exporting some species from the countries of origin. We therefore have two alternatives, namely, to establish breeding centers in this country or to establish preserves or breeding centers in the countries of origin.

CURRENT DOMESTIC BREEDING EFFORTS

Breeding colonies in the United States are currently producing a very small portion of the primates used for research purposes. A recent survey by Thorington (1971) lists 125 active domestic breeding colonies with a total production of some 2200 live births in 1970. Assuming a yearly requirement of 70,000 animals, this represents approximately 3 percent of United States research requirements. There are, however, a number of breeding projects under way or in the planning stage.

The seven Primate Research Centers are striving to become self-sufficient in the breeding of primates for their own use. However, as yet this goal has not been achieved. Breeding colonies of rhesus can be found in most of the Centers and especially in the Oregon, Wisconsin, and California Centers, where they are being used extensively in reproductive biology research. The Washington Center has established an excellent colony of *M. nemestrina* at the Medical Lake Field Station (see Chapter 11 for further discussion of this facility). The New England Center has breeding colonies of four species of macaques for use in a number of their research programs. The Yerkes Center has devoted considerable effort to the breeding of great apes and has been quite successful in breeding chimpanzees and orangutans. The same success is anticipated with gorillas when the colony reaches sexual maturity. The Oregon Center has established breeding colonies of four species of lemurs, and this is probably the only significant breeding colony of these primates in the world. Two rather rare species, *Callicebus moloch* and *Cercopithecus talapoin*, have been established at the Delta Center, and they also plan to initiate breeding colonies of patas and squirrel monkeys.

A number of rather large primate laboratories have been instrumental in establishing breeding colonies in order to provide well-defined animals for research in a number of areas. The Linton Bionetics Research Laboratories, Inc., Kensington, Maryland, is one of the largest breeding centers in the world. During the past 10 years, they have produced some 2100 newborn rhesus and other species for use in cancer chemotherapy and other studies. The Southwest Foundation for Research and Education in San Antonio, Texas, has been responsible for developing much of the information available on the use of the baboon in medical research and has maintained an active breeding colony of these animals for many years. Significant numbers of chimpanzees are being bred at the Holloman Primate Facility in New Mexico and at the Laboratory of Experimental Medicine and Surgery in Primates located in Sterling Forest, New York. In addition, the primate laboratories listed in Table 5 maintain active breeding colonies of the species identified and have made many worthwhile contributions to our knowledge of primate breeding.

There have been two recent developments that hopefully will increase our ability to breed several species of New World primates for domestic biomedical use. The future program of the Caribbean Primate Research Center in Puerto Rico, supported by an NIH contract, calls for the establishment of breeding colonies of several New World species both at the mainland site at Sabana Seca and on the island of La Cueva. Initial efforts will be directed toward the breeding of cebus and owl monkeys. The Gorgas Memorial Laboratory in Panama plans to cooperate with the New England Primate Research Center in establishing breeding colonies of New World species, probably spider and owl monkeys, at the recently acquired Rodman Ammunition Area located in the Canal Zone. This area consists of over 2400 acres of land that is quite similar to the natural habitat of most species found in Central and South America.

The National Institutes of Health have recognized the need for establishing breeding colonies, and in addition to the support provided the laboratories mentioned above, two major steps have been taken to promote primate breeding. Approximately two years ago, the National Institue of Child Health and Human Development surveyed their extramural investigators to ascertain their needs for colony-bred animals in reproductive biology studies. It became clear that the establishment of at least one large breeding colony was essenital if these needs were to be met in the future. A breeding colony of 350 rhesus monkeys has been established under an NIH contract at the California Primate Research Center, and primate materials are being provided to a number of investigators. The Division of Research Resources recognized the importance of determining the costs and feasibility of producing rhesus monkeys on a commercial basis under island or large-enclosure conditions. Recently, an NIH contract has been awarded to the Charles River Laboratories to investigate the commercial feasibility of producing rhesus monkeys on an island off the Florida Keys. This project will be discussed in detail in Chapter 14.

SUMMARY

The needs for colony-bred primates will undoubtedly increase in the future, and it is essential that steps be taken at this time to increase our capabilities of producing sufficient primates of selected species to satisfy our domestic needs. It must not be another situation where too little is done too late.

REFERENCES

Thorington, R. W. (1971). Survey of nonhuman primates being maintained on January 1, 1971. *ILAR News* **15** (1).

CHAPTER 3

Michael A. Nolan

IMPORTING PRIMATES FOR RESEARCH

In recent years, more than 65,000 nonhuman primates have been imported for research use in the United States each year.* This figure excludes imports for the zoological and pet trades. In the average week, therefore, 1200 primates arrive in the United States. Given that an average shipment consists of 100 primates, there are 12 shipments weekly. Of these, approximately 6 arrive in New York, 4 in Miami, and 2 at random points such as Washington, D.C., and Detroit. I would like to comment at this stage on the decrease in the use of primates since the high point in 1962. The reason for this is the change in the use of primates. While more people are using primates, there are less and less acute studies being conducted with primates. The primate is becoming an animal used for studies of chronic disorders, which results in its being conserved. And soon the Division of Biologic Standards is going to change the regulations for producing some vaccines, so that each production lot does not have to be tested, with the animal sacrificed, but only the seed virus need be tested. This is going to cut down considerably on the acute testing of primates, and this simple factor alone will do much to conserve primates. When an animal is being used chronically, often other disciplines can use it during the course of that chronic study. So several disciplines may have the one animal at their disposal, as long as their studies are not in conflict.

---

* See Chapter 2 for more complete statistics on United States primate imports.

THE IMPORT PROCESS

What is involved in the import process? First, you have to alert your suppliers as to what is needed in a given week. A great deal depends on what prior advice your customers have given you, what your "crystal ball" tells you may be needed sometime in the future, and what space will become available to accommodate new arrivals. Of course, for the customer to be able to advise the importer of his needs, he must be able to anticipate the future needs of projects requiring monkeys. It is always amazing to me that institutions that can project their rodent needs for months (and, in fact, years) in advance have trouble knowing from day to day what numbers and species of primates will be needed within a week.

It goes without saying that a reliable network of suppliers is essential. These have to be spread throughout the primate world, from Djakarta, Indonesia, to Lima, Peru.

After advising the supplier, it is necessary to schedule appropriate flights so that the primates arrive during the working week and, hopefully, during the working day. The United States Government has a requirement that all primates must be delivered between the hours of 8 a.m. and 5 p.m. Transportation is a very significant factor in primates. First, you have to either get them or produce them. Second, you have to *transport* them. Third, you have to apply preventive medicine to them. Fourth, investigators receive them. But without proper transportation methods even if there were a domestic source of production, forget it; they do not travel well by boxcar.

These flights must be planned so that groups and species of monkeys are separated not only by aircraft, but also by time and geography. For example, if you have a shipment of, say, squirrel monkeys from Lima, you do not want on the same aircraft, in the same hold, a shipment of squirrel monkeys from Brazil, even though they are the same species. The mere fact that they are from separate geographical areas means that they have a separate flora, and when you mix that up (and I am not a scientist but I know from experience), the result can be disastrous.

When the primates arrive at the gateway airport, a series of inspections of both the animals and the documentation are carried out by the U.S. Public Health Service, the Department of Agriculture, the Fish and Wildlife Service of the Department of the Interior, and finally the U.S. Customs. (This includes everybody but the Internal Revenue people; they get in on it later on.) A normal clearance time in accomplishing the import paper work and the inspections averages 4 hours. There is an invariable rule: when the weight of the papers equals the weight of the monkeys, the shipment is ready for delivery. It is important to accomplish this before 5 p.m., since agency inspectors either may not be available or available only at prohibitive overtime rates.

Then comes the disposition of the primates. Some groups will go directly to the customers by connecting flights. This depends entirely on the user. Some users have an extreme interest in avoiding cross-contamination by unwanted viruses. And in that case, they do not want those primates waiting any longer in one area than is absolutely necessary. The quicker the animal gets from the tree to their facility, the better for their study. The majority of the animals, however, have to be accommodated in the importer's quarantine facility. Believe me, nothing causes ulcers quicker than having only 50 available spaces to accommodate 100 primates that require individual caging! An an anecdote, to go back a few years: I got a Christmas present one Christmas Eve. The supplier took advantage of an unscheduled flight that arrived on Christmas Eve at 5 p.m. with 250 primates, and needless to say, my Christmas dinner had to wait awhile.

THE CHANGING NEEDS FOR PRIMATES

There have been obvious changes in the nature of primates used for research over the past 10 years. There has been a species shift: tamarins/marmosets have become very important in virology because of their susceptibility to most viruses; baboons are being used more in surgical research. In fact, the diversity of needs is one of the problems in the domestic breeding of primates. Today's need for rhesus may be tomorrow's need for owls, tomorrow's need for owls may be the next day's need for chimpanzees. You never can anticipate! Therefore, your domestic breeding program, even if it is only to encompass the more commonly used primates, has to be a vast enterprise. It cannot be just for one species, because as soon as you develop that one species you will find that nobody wants to use it because somebody has discovered another latent virus in it and has negated its value.

The rhesus macaque, however, is still used more frequently than all other species combined—close to 60 percent. The reason for this is simple. There is a vast background of knowledge on the use of this primate and precedent is a mighty persuader. The rhesus is everybody's second choice; he would make a wonderful vice president.

The most significant shift is in the variety of disciplines now using primates, which has given rise to a host of differing specifics required of the importer. We have to hold about three times the number of animals we sell monthly because of this very reason. It used to be true that orders were facsimiles of each other, for example, "100 juvenile rhesus, no weight requirement." One day recently, we shipped out 15 baboons, 2 chimpanzees, 35 squirrel monkeys, 60 rhesus, 3 pig-tails, and 12 cynomolgus to 18 different customers. Also within this diversity was an equal variance of age, sex, and size requirements, with such specific characteristics as "eyes without cataracts," "adult dentition, without erupted third molars," "no tetracycline medication," and so on. The "third-molar" requirement is based on the rule-of-thumb that a rhesus monkey is adult when it has its third molars. Therefore investigators want "rhesus females with fully erupted third molars which are not over four years old," and that request is difficult to fulfill. To service such requests it is imperative to have the animals on hand, in good condition, and inspected by a competent veterinarian. And, in fact, I feel strongly about the veterinary inspection. One of the things I like about the trend in these meetings is that an importer used to come to a primate meeting and have a number of behavioral scientists telling him what he did wrong. Now we have a number of veterinarians telling us what we do wrong, but they are more equipped to do so.

THE PROBLEMS OF SUPPLIERS

To this point we have concentrated on the importing country and its problems and trends. What about the supplying countries? There, the equation is more complex. I believe the exporting countries, with few exceptions, will value the incoming foreign currencies more than religious, academic, or political prejudice. However, there is the danger of diminishing supplies. One case is the chimpanzee, which I feel strongly should no longer be brought from abroad, but should be supplied by a national chimpanzee center in this country. It is a regret that Holloman Air Force Base was not developed for that. It is unfortunate that they are not producing chimpanzees, because they *can* produce chimpanzees but have not gotten the recognition as a supply source for chimpanzees. If I were a lobbyist, I would lobby for that very strongly. Given that not more than 200 chimpanzees are required annually, it should not be difficult to fulfill this requirement through domestic production, provided that the significant financial support required is forthcoming. From the businessman's point of view, the chimpanzee is another piece of merchandise; but as somebody pointed out, if we keep using up our merchandise, pretty soon we will not have any merchandise to sell. And with the chimpanzee, I would be quite willing to forego selling that animal. I recognize that this attitude is strictly that of a conservationist.

CIVILIZATION AND THE DESTRUCTION OF HABITAT

Another case is more imperative—that of the population explosion overwhelming the habitat of the primate. To emphasize, it is not so much the export of the monkeys or the trapping of them, it is the absolute envelopment of their habitats by people wanting to farm the land. This is very evident, for example, in the Philippines where farming and timber harvesting have decimated the rain forests of Mindanao. With the coming approach of the Brazilian trans-Amazon highway, the same situation is probable for that area. While Brazil does not officially export South American monkeys, a number of South American monkeys that are theoretically from other countries actually come from Brazil, which is a vast reservoir. In situations such as this, the monkey population has a very poor chance of expanding. This is, I think, the greatest single danger. It may also be a danger in the ranching of monkeys, because in order to ranch monkeys you must have a vast area, you must contain them within that area, and that area may be very desirable for farming. How that can be solved, I do not know.

CONCLUSION

It is conceivable that within 25 years the overseas supplies will have to be vigorously supplemented by a domestic breeding program. The Animal Resources Branch of the U.S. National Institutes of Health has directed itself toward that situation and will, hopefully, come up with some answers to the economics of it. The actual mechanics are relatively simple, except for the containment of the primates. The only uncertainty I would have about such a program is how to take care of the diversity of needs mentioned above.

CHAPTER 4

Kenneth T. Kirton

NEEDS OF THE PHARMACEUTICAL INDUSTRY FOR EXPERIMENTAL PRIMATES

My charge for this conference was to assess future needs of the pharmaceutical industry for experimental primates. As is always the case, predictions for the future are difficult to make and the accuracy of such predictions is subject to alterations caused by unforeseen changes in inputs or demands. In trying to predict future needs, it seems that there are two parameters that must be weighed to achieve a net result, namely, trends in past demands (use) and changing trends based on future demands. One of these, recent trends in use, is quite easily obtainable. The other is more difficult to predict and accounts for most of the variation in terms of future predictions.

The total number of primates imported by the United States has been compiled by the Institute of Laboratory Animal Resources (ILAR). These totals are available for each of the last several years and are illustrated in Table 1. The trend over the past four years appears to be an almost linear decrease with time. Undoubtedly this decrease will eventually level off; it is only a matter of when and thus at which level. There is some evidence that such an adjustment has now taken place, at about 40,000 primates a year. The decrease in numbers of primates imported during the past few years is attributable to decreases in the number of both Old and New World primates imported, thus indicating a gener-

Table 1   Primates Imported by the United States[a]

Species	Year			
	1968	1969	1970	1971
African Green	5,262	5,852	3,011	
Rhesus	37,290	34,665	27,092	
Total (Old World)	50,265	49,148	38,387	
Total primates	85,283	68,002	54,433	48,660

[a] Source: Institute of Laboratory Animal Resources Newsletter.

alized decrease in demand for primates. This decrease has been paralleled by a similar reduction in the numbers of primates used by pharmaceutical companies (Table 2) and by the numbers used by contract research corporations that work in direct support of pharmaceutical companies (Table 3). When these two totals are added to obtain an index of total

Table 2   Numbers of Primates Used by Pharmaceutical Companies

Company	Year			
	1968	1969	1970	1971
1	1,152	8	105	12
2	50	60	45	50
3	73	121	153	207
4	114	67	58	65
5	8	194	97	94
6	50	46	57	152
7	57	37	48	53
Total	1,504	533	563	733

Table 3   Primates Used by Contract Research Organizations in Support of Pharmaceutical Industry

Contractor	Year			
	1968	1969	1970	1971
1	4,000[a]	4,289	3,526	1,702
2	11,622	10,511	8,834	5,487
3	—	66	416	636
4	40	26	37	25
Total	15,662	14,892	12,813	7,850

[a] Estimated.

Table 4   Percentage of Total United States Primates Imported for Pharmaceutical Industry Use[a]

	Year			
	1968	1969	1970	1971
Total U.S. imports	85,283	68,002	54,433	48,660
Those for pharmaceutical use	16,166	15,425	13,376	8,583
Percent of total	19	22	24	17

[a] The figures given here are based on the responses of 7 out of 12 pharmaceutical companies surveyed.

pharmaceutical use, one comes up with a trend that has about equaled the changes in total numbers of primates imported (Table 4). This trend can be expected to continue in the future, with the possibility of a gradual shift to a larger percentage of the total animals being imported slated for pharmaceutical purposes.

The total primate uses by the pharmaceutical industry, in terms of absolute numbers, are somewhat difficult to ascertain. A survey of six principal commercial primate importers indicated that between 30 and 50 percent of the total animals imported each year were for use by the pharmaceutical industry. The figures given in Table 4 are certainly minimum estimates, since not all users were tabulated. Of 12 pharmaceutical companies queried, 7 responses were received. In general, an opinion was expressed by those surveyed that the pharmaceutical use of primates was declining due to the recent reduction in primate uses for production of vaccines. This decline will no doubt be offset in the future by an increasing trend in primate usage for basic research and for toxicology in support of new drug development. As an example, a recent article (Djerassi, 1970) suggested that development of a new male antifertility agent would require support toxicology studies in 500 primates, and 5400 primates would be needed for development of a luteolytic or abortifacient agent! Similar increased uses could be expected for other aspects of the industry, particularly cardiovascular, central nervous system, and similar areas of pharmaceutical research where significant differences in animal species warrant the use of primates. Additional emphasis on primate use is being stimulated by the recognition by regulatory authorities of the validity of primates as experimental models. These areas of research use primarily the rhesus monkey and can be expected to continue predominantly with this species in the future.

As more basic research is conducted with primates, more and more significant differences appear between primates and subprimate species. These differences then would seem to justify a continued use of large numbers of primates for basic research purposes, upon which basic drug development plans could be based.

The validity of these studies is, of course, no better than the quality of experimental animal used. In the past, many of the primates imported into this country have been less than ideal for use as research animals. The difficulties—disease, parasites, and so on—are partly present prior to capture and partly developed after capture during shipment to the domestic site of use. In addition, age and, for the most part, past reproductive history are unknown for animals trapped in the wild. These difficulties could be circumvented by the use of animals raised domestically, where accurate records and standardized conditions of care could be maintained. These advantages would seem to outweigh any disadvantage in terms of increased cost of raising and need for placing orders at longer intervals prior to expected delivery.

At the present time, most of the cost of an experimental primate is acquired after it has been purchased from an importer. An average initial cost for a mature rhesus female is \$50–\$70. Costs on a per diem basis for maintenance are \$1.15–\$1.40, and the period of quarantine and acclimatization of two to six months is required following arrival. This then would add between \$70 and \$250 to the cost of an experimental animal acquired and handled under present methods of importation. This results in a total investment of at least \$120 and as much as \$320 for an animal ready for physiological experimentation. The initial purchase price of animals raised in a domestic environment would undoubtedly be higher than for animals trapped in their native habitat and imported under current conditions. However, the advantages of animals from a domestic source would be: a reduced investment in time for quarantine and acclimatization, the probability of healthier animals, and the availability of a more complete medical history. These advantages would seem to offset the disadvantages of increased initial purchase price and a possible longer lag time from initial requisition to delivery.

REFERENCES

Djerassi, C. (1970). Birth control after 1984. *Science* 169:941.

CHAPTER 5

Charles H. Southwick
M. Rafiq Siddiqi
M. Farooq Siddiqi

PRIMATE POPULATIONS AND BIOMEDICAL RESEARCH*†

Declining primate populations throughout the world represent serious losses for biomedical research. The great value of nonhuman primates in biomedical research is clearly established, and so also is the need for a wide range of species from which investigators can select the best models. It is obvious that no single primate species can serve all research interests, nor can the scientific community fully predict which species may be key models in a particular problem. Several years ago we did not know that the night or owl monkey would become a vital model for the study of human malaria (Voller et al., 1969). Nor did we know that a herpes virus from a squirrel monkey, when inoculated into marmosets, would provide one of the best models of a viral tumor in primates (Melendez et al., 1970; Hunt et al., 1970). The systematic utilization of

* This paper is adapted from a report made to the Advisory Council of the Institute of Laboratory Animal Resources, National Academy of Sciences-National Research Council, on December 11, 1969, and from a speech presented February 7, 1970, in Chicago before the National Society for Medical Research.
† This paper appeared in *Science*, Vol. 170, December 4, 1970, pp. 1051–1054. (Copyright 1970 by the American Association for the Advancement of Science.) It is reprinted here in its entirety, with permission from the authors and *Science*.

primates in biomedical research is at a very early stage in terms of its potential development.

The greatest danger in this development now is that the world's fauna is disappearing at an increasing rate. Since A.D. 1600, at least 120 major species of birds and mammals have become extinct—a rate several times higher than the natural rate of extinction. At present, about one vertebrate species per year is becoming extinct, and probably more than 100 will disappear from the earth in the next 30 to 50 years. The International Union for the Conservation of Nature (IUCN), a scientific organization concerned with the preservation and wise utilization of wildlife and natural resources, now lists 275 species of mammals and 300 species of birds as rare and endangered (IUCN, 1970). There are 49 species and subspecies of primates on the IUCN list of endangered mammals. This is more than 10 percent of all living primate species.

ECOLOGIC VULNERABILITY OF PRIMATES

Primates are in special jeopardy for several reasons. In the first place, most primate species are forest inhabitants and are especially vulnerable to worldwide patterns of deforestation, slash-and-burn agriculture, herbicide application, and jungle warfare which occur in many of the world's tropical forests. Reforestation, for example, may affect primates deleteriously because of the extensive trend in Asia and Latin America to reforest with single-species stands, especially eucalyptus. Eucalyptus plantings are popular because of their rapid growth and high productivity, but they are of very little value as food or cover for primates or other forest dwellers.

Second, most primates are graminivorous and frugivorous and are in direct competition with human populations around villages and agricultural lands. The villagers of India, for example, have become decreasingly tolerant of rhesus monkeys and have encouraged the trapping and removal of monkeys from agricultural lands.

Third, in many of the forested hill regions of Asia, throughout peninsular Asia, and in parts of Indonesia, monkeys are now commonly hunted by the indigenous populations for food and as a source of medicinal or magic potions made from the bones and various organs. Changing social mores of the peoples of Asia are eroding the "sacred image" of the monkey and account for a lessening of one-time stringently protective attitudes.

Finally, primates are being trapped in increasing numbers for commercial use. Both the pet trade and biomedical research take large numbers of primates in international commerce. More than 50,000 primates are used for research each year in the United States alone.

Habitat deterioration, pressure of human populations, changing human attitudes, hunting, and trapping—these forces combined threaten to decimate primate populations throughout the world. Already, several primate species are approaching extinction.

It is apparent that primate populations can become extinct even in areas where primates are greatly honored and revered. The gibbon (*Hylobates lar*) played a vital role in the art, history, dance, music, and entire cultural heritage of China for more than 2000 years, and was formerly abundant throughout China as far north as the Yellow River and as far west as Chengtu and Lanchow. By the year 1644, the gibbon had become so rare in China that it ceased from this date to figure in the literature, art, and music of the culture; since then it has been of only historical importance (Van Gulik, 1967). Even though the gibbon was endowed, in the culture of ancient China, with wisdom and mystical powers and had a semireligious role, it still became extinct throughout the country. We shall never know all the reasons for this extinction, but it probably occurred with the deforestation of China and the destruction of the gibbon's habitat.

From an ecologic viewpoint, an extinction of any desirable animal means a decrease in faunal diversity, hence a decrease in ecosystem stability. From a biomedical viewpoint, each extinction means the loss of a unique source of biological material. It becomes increasingly incumbent upon mankind in general, and upon the scientific community in particular, to undertake more vigorous research and conservation programs to protect endangered primates. Conservation means more than strict protectionism. It means wise use and planned management, based on scientific knowledge.

PATTERNS OF PRIMATE UTILIZATION

With these basic premises in mind, let us consider several aspects of the current situation regarding the supply of primates. There are at least three broad patterns.

1. In the case of some species, such as the rhesus, the African green monkey, the squirrel monkey, and the Java or cynomolgus macaque, there is heavy utilization of abundant populations. These populations may or may not be able to sustain present levels of harvest.

2. Other species are utilized to only a moderate degree for research, but they are less abundant and are feeling the pressure both of a deteriorating environment and of wasteful trapping or shooting. In this category are the stump-tailed macaque, the pig-tailed macaque, some of the marmosets, and the owl or night monkey.

3. Still other species are used very little for research at present, but are in serious danger of extinction due to a loss of limited habitat, waste in nonscientific commercial trade, and the fact that they are rare to begin with. In this category are the lion-tailed macaque of India, the douc langur, the golden marmoset, the red *Colobus*, some of the lemurs, and the orangutan.

In most of these situations there is a lack of scientific knowledge about the true status of the population and the basic population dynamics. It is not necessarily wise, and is probably dangerous at this stage, to be unduly alarmist about the fate of all these species, but it is equally dangerous to be complacent about those that are not dramatically near extinction. We cannot put all the above species into a single list of rare and endangered species, nor can we urge for all of them a program of total protectionism. For example, the rhesus and bonnet macaques cannot be considered rare and endangered at present, although populations of the former have been declining markedly. We have virtually no knowledge about *Macaca fascicularis* or *M. maura* populations and cannot plan intelligent management programs for these species at this time. On the other hand, we do know that *M. silenus* is in serious danger and needs immediate attention and that *M. speciosa* is in a relatively poor situation and also requires strict conservation attention (Bertrand, 1969). *Macaca silenus*, the lion-tailed macaque, is not utilized in research, but, due to its unique position as the only truly arboreal macaque, it may at some time become the vital model for a biological problem, and when that day arrives it may be too late. Sugiyama (1968) estimated several years ago that the total population of lion-tailed macaques consisted of no more than 1000 animals, and the number is now probably less than that. The common pig-tailed macaque in Malaya has been diminishing markedly under human predation (Bernstein, 1967), and we do not know the true population status or production rate.

In December of 1969, one of us (Southwick) stopped in Burma for a few days in hopes of finding rich populations of macaques there. Burma has been closed to Western animal traders for 20 years, and it is the only nation in Southeast Asia that has never trapped or exported monkeys commercially. In three days of fieldwork in the forests of Pegu, northeast of Rangoon, Southwick found no monkeys and was told that the villagers and hill people shoot them for food and medicinal potions. There are undoubtedly some macaques in the region, but certainly they do not occur in the abundance expected.

RHESUS POPULATIONS IN INDIA

Several principles of primate population ecology and utilization can be illustrated with data on rhesus macaques (Figure 1) in India, gathered over the last 10 years. In September 1959, we began a systematic program of population study in Aligarh District of Western Uttar Pradesh in northern India, in which we have censused some 17 groups of wild

Figure 1.   Rhesus monkey, female and young (*Macaca mulatta*).

rhesus every 4 months for 10 years. We are citing this, not as a model study or even an entirely adequate one, but as one representing some of the types of data that are needed to evaluate primate population ecology.

Our first year's work showed that the rhesus populations of northern India were declining in the late 1950s and early 1960s, due to at least three causes. First, most of the villagers were becoming less tolerant of crop depredations by monkeys and were anxious to rid their area of monkeys. We knew of many instances of villagers trapping or killing rhesus monkeys to save their crops. Second, trapping for export was taking a very large toll throughout the late 1950s—over 100,000 animals per year, and in some years over 200,000. This was producing a conspicuous change in the age structure of the rhesus population, reducing the relative numbers of juvenile monkeys (Southwick, Beg, and Siddiqi, 1965). Third, changes in land use were adversely affecting rhesus populations; these changes included deforestation and single-species reforestation, that is, the replacing of mixed deciduous forests with pure stands of sal (*Shorea robusta*) and eucalyptus, which are less favorable as rhesus habitat.

Through 1964, 1965, and 1966 our population studies showed a continued population decline in rhesus groups in village, roadside, and rural habitats (Figures 2 and 3). Forest populations seemed to be stabilizing,

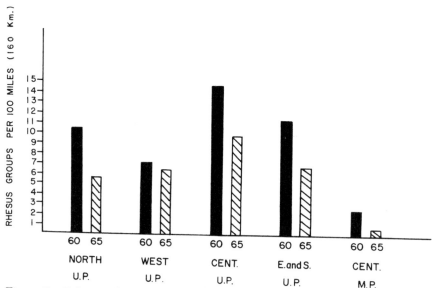

Figure 2. Relative abundance of roadside groups of rhesus in various regions of northern India, 1960 and 1965. U.P.: Uttar Pradesh; M.P.: Madhya Pradesh.

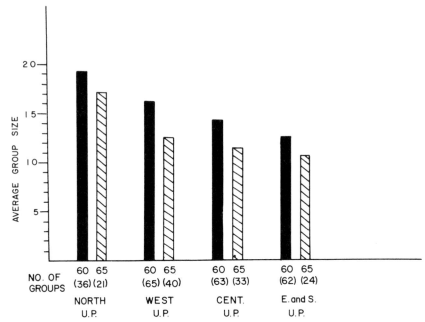

Figure 3.   Relative group sizes of roadside groups of rhesus in various regions of northern India, 1960 and 1965. U.P.: Uttar Pradesh; M. P.: Madhya Pradesh. Values in parentheses are numbers of groups.

and town populations were increasing in some areas (Southwick and Siddiqi, 1966; 1968). All populations were showing better age structures, with substantial increases in the juvenile age component. The percentages of juveniles had increased from 5 percent or less to 15–20 percent in many habitats. Trapping for export had declined substantially, to less than 50,000 per year.

Our most recent data indicate that a decline in population is still occurring in villages and rural areas, due primarily to cultural and economic forces, but that forest populations may be reaching a more stable level and that urban monkeys* may still be increasing in certain

* Urban monkeys, as distinct from forest dwellers, are groups resident in cities, towns, and villages. They frequent temple areas, railway stations, roadsides leading into the cities, and bazaars. While generally tolerated by people, urban monkeys (outside of temple areas) are often threatened or disturbed in crowded areas. The monkeys in temple grounds are fed and partially protected by local people, yet temple rhesus are more aggressive than forest-dwelling rhesus.

areas. This is not necessarily desirable, because urban monkeys are in relatively poor health, having a high incidence of respiratory and enteric disease, and are a nuisance rather than a valuable animal resource.

Our original Aligarh District population of rural rhesus monkeys, which in 1959 consisted of 17 social groups totaling 337 monkeys, increased to a peak of 23 groups and 403 monkeys in 1962, but since then has shown an erratic decline to the point where it now (in March 1970) numbers only 13 groups and 163 monkeys. Only two of the original 17 groups received protection from the local villagers. These groups have been relatively stable, whereas all the others have declined (Figure 4).

Our current estimates on the population size and productivity of the rhesus of Uttar Pradesh indicate a population in the neighborhood of 500,000 animals (of which approximately 43 percent are adult females), with an excellent birthrate of 82 percent. We estimate that this population is producing 176,000 infants per year, of which nearly 60,000 could be harvested if certain other ecologic forces were not operative. We feel that planned management of the rhesus population of India could theo-

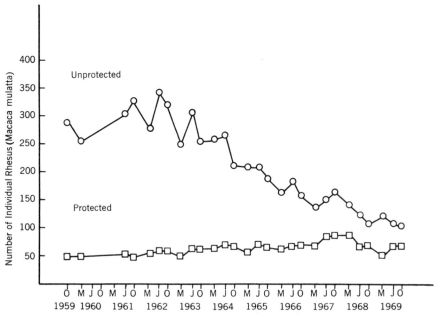

Figure 4.   Trends in populations of unprotected and protected rhesus in Aligarh District, Uttar Pradesh, northern India, 1959 to 1969. Census counts: O: October; M: March; J: July.

retically maintain a substantial harvest, without further diminution. But it is difficult at this stage to predict how extensive future changes in habitat will be and how much more the Indian peoples' traditional habits of protecting monkeys will erode. With these multiple factors affecting the rhesus population adversely, we feel that further decline is likely. More emphasis should be placed on monkeys as important national and international resources and less on monkeys as agricultural pests. They should receive careful scientific and managerial attention as major renewable resources.

Even though the rhesus monkey is one of the primate species that has been most thoroughly studied under laboratory and field conditions, there are several aspects of its basic ecology that have never been investigated. To the best of our knowledge no adequate study of the distribution of the rhesus throughout India and Pakistan has ever been made; there has never been a detailed field study made of its food habits in different habitats [except for D. G. Lindburg's (1971) field studies on the ecology and behavior of forest groups around Dehra Dun and M. K. Neville's (1968) observation around Haldwani]; and there has been remarkably little study of natural diseases in wild rhesus. Our own research is no more than a beginning on what should be done in the area of rhesus population ecology.

RESEARCH NEEDS AND CONSERVATION STRATEGY

We believe there is a danger of undue emotionalism about primate conservation before adequate field data are available. It is likely that biomedical research will receive the brunt of blame for many problems. When shortages of primates occur, the most convenient and visible scapegoat is the research laboratory. We are the first to admit that excessive harvesting of primate populations may be detrimental, but we also think that other ecologic and social forces are equally detrimental and, in the long run, more serious. The greatest threat to primate populations throughout the world is alteration of the environment, through deforestation, slash-and-burn agriculture, poaching, jungle warfare, food shortages, and excessive utilization of herbicides and defoliants.

For the research community, the practical problem right now is to attach the blame for attrition of primate populations where it belongs: on these corrosive conditions and practices. It is imperative to secure sound field data in quantity, to bring into more exact focus the true ecologic picture, and to support with this increased flow of data a new thrust in the management of a wise course of conservation practices and programs.

Another danger in excessive alarm is the possibility that some countries may prohibit all export of primates, considering this adequate protection. This would end the activities of legitimate dealers, those with the best and most humane programs, and would stimulate undesirable illegal trade. It could accelerate losses and damage to primate populations by driving the business underground and taking it out of the arena of legitimate governmental and scientific regulation. It would divert attention from the real needs of habitat conservation and scientific management.

At present our most critical need is to obtain data on the population status, trends, and reproductive biology of primates that are used in biomedical research or that represent endangered species. We know little or nothing about the population status of squirrel monkeys, owl monkeys, marmosets, pig-tailed macaques, cynomolgus macaques, rock macaques, gibbons, vervets, talapoin monkeys, and several other species of primates that are already important in research.* There has been a great flurry of field studies on primates in the last 15 years, but these have been primarily behavioral in nature, and the entire subject of primate population ecology has been neglected.

Although use of primates in research may level out or even decline for a few years, the long-term demand will certainly increase. In the meantime, the inexorable forces of ecology will operate on indigenous primate populations, and they most certainly will be detrimental.

We feel that two major types of programs should be initiated as soon as possible: (1) a coordinated and well-planned program of population research to provide more accurate data on the ecologic status and reproductive biology of important species of primates, and (2) active conservation programs for all endangered species and all species that are directly utilized in biomedical research. The population surveys are necessary to provide the data on which sound conservation practices can be based. The conservation programs are essential to insure that some of the world's important primate species will still be here 10 years from now.

ACKNOWLEDGMENTS

We are indebted to M. A. Beg, R. K. Lahiri, M. Bertrand, P. Jay, D. G. Lindburg, M. K. Neville, and R. P. Mukherjee for field assistance; to M.

---

* Since this was written in 1970, several major studies of some of these species have been undertaken and will be published in the near future.

B. Mirza, J. L. Bhaduri, F. B. Bang, C. Wallace, A. Craemer, R. Yager, H. Kingman, and N. Alim for administrative support; and to B. Harrisson for reading the manuscript.

REFERENCES

Bernstein, I. S. (1967). A field study of the pigtail monkey (*Macaca nemestrina*). *Primates* 8:217.

Bertrand, M. (1969). The behavioral repertoire of the stumptail macaque. *Bibliotheca Primatologica* 11:273.

Hunt, R. D., Melendez, L. V., King, N. W., Gilmore, C. E., Daniel, M. D., Williamson, M. E., and Jones, R. C. (1970). Morphology of a disease with features of malignant lymphoma in marmosets and owl monkeys inoculated with *Herpesvirus saimiri. Journal of the National Cancer Institute* 44:447–466.

Lindburg, D. G. (1971). The rhesus monkey in north India: an ecological and behavioral study. In L. A. Rosenblum (Ed.), *Primate behavior: Developments in field and laboratory research.* Vol. 2. New York: Academic Press, pp. 1–106.

Neville, M. K. (1968). Ecology and activity of Himalayan foothill rhesus monkeys. *Ecology* 49:110–123.

Melendez, L. V., Daniel, M. D., Hunt, R. D., Fraser, C. E. O., Garcia, F. G., King, N. W., and Williamson, M. E. (1970). *Herpesvirus saimiri.* V: Further evidence to consider this virus as the etiologic agent of a lethal disease in primates which resembles a malignant lymphoma. *Journal of the National Cancer Institute* 44: 1175–1182.

Southwick, C. H., Beg, M. A., and Siddiqi, M. R. (1965). Chap. 4. In I. DeVore (Ed.), *Primate behavior.* Toronto: Holt, pp. 111–159.

Southwick, C. H., and Siddiqi, M. R. (1966). Population change of rhesus monkeys (*Macaca mulatta*) in India 1959–1965. *Primates* 7:303..

——— (1968). Population trends of rhesus monkeys in villages and towns of northern India. *Journal of Animal Ecology,* 37:199.

Sugiyama, Y. (1968). The ecology of the lion-tailed macaque—a pilot study. *Journal of the Bombay Natural History Society* 65:283.

Survival Service Commission (1970). *Red data book.* Morges, Switzerland: IUCN.

Van Gulik, R. H. (1967). *The gibbon in China.* Leiden, Netherlands: Brill.

Voller, A., Hawkey, C. M., Richards, W. H., and Ridley, D. S. (1969). Human malaria (*Plasmodium falciparum*) in owl monkeys (*Aotus trivirgatus*). *Journal of Tropical Medicine and Hygiene* 72:153.

CHAPTER 6

Robert W. Cooper
Jorge Hernandez-Camacho

A CURRENT APPRAISAL OF COLOMBIA'S PRIMATE RESOURCES

COLOMBIA'S FAUNAL RESOURCES

The first serious use of Neotropical primates in a biomedical research area was probably in the investigation of yellow fever (Bates, 1944; Bates and Roca-Garcia, 1945; Bates and Roca-Garcia, 1946; Davis, 1930; Laemmert, 1944). Much of this early work was conducted in Colombia by Marston Bates and his collaborator Manuel Roca-Garcia under the auspices of what was then the Ministry of Labor, Hygiene and Social Welfare of the Republic of Colombia and of the International Health Division of the Rockefeller Foundation. And today, while closely following Peru as the principal exporter of New World primates, Colombia is by far the leading supplier of such species for biomedical research (Clarkson, 1971).

Because Colombia is also a large supplier of other faunal forms both as live specimens and as crude and tanned skins, it is perhaps of value to place the primate trade in this broader perspective. As indicated in Table 1, in 1970 Colombia produced for export over 1 million animal units, of which 61 percent represented specimens exploited for their skins.* The major skin-producing species are listed in the table, with the spectacled caiman (*Caiman crocodilus*) being by far the leader.

---

* All animal exportation statistics given in this paper were taken from the *Anuario de la Fauna Silvestre en Colombia—1970*, INDERENA (Institute for the Development of Renewable Natural Resources), Oficina de Planeacion, 1971.

Table 1   Total Colombian Faunal Exports—1970

Exported Item	Units	Export Value (U.S. $)
Wild animal skins		
Reptiles and Amphibians		
Spectacled caiman		
(*Caiman crocodilus*)	603,145	2,243,020
Tegu lizards		
(*Tupinambis* sp.)	51,030	43,380
Toads (*Bufo marinus*)	22,000	6,600
Iguanas (*I. iguana iguana*)	6,100	2,790
Boas (*Boa constrictor* and		
Eunectes murinus)	2,841	36,679
Crocodiles (*Crocodylus* spp. and		
Melanusuchus niger)	2,633	38,330
Snakes (unidentified)	1,000	6,000
Total reptile and amphibian skins	688,749	2,376,799
Mammals		
Collared peccary (*Dicotyles tajacu*)	55,486	92,895
Spotted cats (mainly *Felis pardalis,*		
F. tigrina, and *F. wiedii*)	27,094	1,016,119
Capybara (*Hydrochaeris hydrochaeris*)	25,960	47,245
White-lipped peccary		
(*Tayassu pecari*)	17,883	20,896
River otter (*Lutra longicaudis*)	5,573	112,557
Deer (*Mazama americana* and		
Odocoileus virginianus)	2,676	6,690
Jaguar (*Felis onca*)	1,387	212,245
Giant otter (*Pteronura brasiliensis*)	297	17,525
Total mammal skins	136,356	1,526,172
Total wild animal skins	825,105	3,902,971
(Total skins exported to U.S.)	(501,467)	(2,294,465)
Live animals		
Reptiles and Amphibians		
Lizards		
Baby and juvenile iguanas		
(*I. iguana iguana*)	136,993	34,411
Other small lizards of		
the family Iguanidae	39,902	9,950
Lizards of the family Teiidae	43,065	21,727

Table 1 (continued)

Exported Item	Units	Export Value (U.S. $)
Snakes		
Boas (largely young of		
Boa constrictor)	11,177	25,296
Rattlesnakes	755	11,190
Snakes (unidentified)	15,595	60,663
Turtles		
Tortoises (*Geochelone* spp.)	7,461	6,594
Turtles (mainly baby		
Chrysemys scripta and		
Podocnemis spp.)	152,613	33,745
Crocodilians		
Caiman crocodilus (baby)	200	60
Crocodylus sp. and		
Melanosuchus niger (young)	429	370
Amphibians		
Toads (largely *Bufo marinus*)	44,818	14,980
Frogs	1,536	326
Total reptiles and amphibians	454,544	218,312
Birds		
Macaws, parrots, and parakeets		
(largely *Ara* sp., *Amazona* spp.,		
Brotogeris jugularis, and		
Forpus spp.)	34,155	218,950
Passarine cage species		
(mainly various finches,		
tanagers, and orioles)	16,714	13,318
Toucans (*Ramphastos* spp. and		
Pteroglossus spp.)	3,277	34,791
Hawks and eagles	2,291	10,908
Miscellaneous (e.g., *Chauna*		
chavaria, *Psophia crepitans*,		
Pelecanus occidentalis, and		
Sarcoramphus papa)	160	1,267
Total birds	56,597	279,234
Mammals		
Primates (see primate section below)	16,380	107,981
Carnivores (largely *Procyon*		
spp., *Potos*, *Nasua*, and		
Felis spp.)	1,535	16,399

Table 1 (continued)

Exported Item	Units	Export Value (U.S. $)
Edentates (largely *Tamandua*, *Myrmecophaga*, and *Choloepus*)	547	3,228
Rodents (largely *Hydrochaeris*, *Dasyprocta*, and *Agouti*)	149	436
Marsupials (largely *Marmosa* and *Caluromys*)	116	192
Perissodactyles and artiodactyles (*Tapirus* and *Tayassu*)	13	565
Total mammals	18,740	128,801
Total animals	529,881	626,347
(Total animals exported to U.S.)	(303,069)	(351,353)
Total Colombian skin and live animal exports, 1970	1,354,986	4,529,318
(Total skin and live animal exports to U.S., 1970)	(804,536)	(2,645,818)
Primates		
Squirrel monkey (*Saimiri sciureus*)	5,563	24,832
Night or owl monkey (*Aotus trivirgatus*)	2,825	15,701
Marmosets or tamarins (largely *Saguinus oedipus, S. mystax,* and *S. nigricollis*)	2,090	6,844
Woolly monkey (*Lagothrix lagothricha*)	305	9,678
Capuchin monkeys (*Cebus albifrons, C. capucinus,* and *C. apella*)	264	2,833
Spider monkeys (*Ateles paniscus hybridus, A.p. robustus,* and *A.p. belzebuth*)	115	1,293
Red uakari (*Cacajao rubicundus*)	20	277
Titi monkeys (*Callicebus moloch* and *C. torquatus*)	46	470
Saki monkey (*Pithecia monachus*)	18	76
Red howler monkey (*Alouatta seniculus*)	1	3
Others without identification (largely *Cebus* spp., *Saguinus* spp., *Aotus,* and *Ateles p.* sbspp.)	5,133	45,974
Total primates	16,380	107,032
(Total primates exported to U.S.)	(15,382)	(101,032)

Of the recorded total numbers of live animals exported, 86 percent were reptiles and amphibians, such as baby iguanas, other iguanid and teiid lizards, turtles and tortoises, snakes, and toads. Birds totaled approximately 10.5 percent of live animals exported, and of the mammal exportations (3.5 percent) the vast majority were primates. The non-primate mammals included relatively small numbers of carnivores, edentates, rodents, and marsupials.

We are uncertain about the accuracy of the specific exportation numbers of the various primates listed in the table, partly because of the additional 1970 primate statistical export category of "monkeys without identification" totaling 31.3 percent of all primate exports. Further insight into the concordance of Colombian (export) and United States (import) statistics on the trade in Colombian primates for 1970 can be gained from comparing INDERENA export data with the U.S. Department of Interior import statistics of Paradiso and Fisher (1972).

The total estimated value of Colombia's 1970 faunistic exportation is based on skin-producing and live animals, but excludes both aquarium and meat fishes. The total value of primates exported represents less than 2.4 percent of all faunistic income and an average of US $6.60 per primate specimen. The list of countries to which Colombia supplies both animal skins and live animal specimens is rather long, including representatives of every continent. However, the United States is presently the dominant market for Colombian faunal resources; for example, the value of skins exported to the United States in 1970 was about 58 percent of all Colombian skin exportations. In addition, the reported value of live animals purchased by the United States was 56 percent of all foreign sales for that year. And the value of primates shipped to the United States was an overwhelming 93.7 percent of total Colombian primate exports.

Combining the fact that primate exports represent less than 3 percent of Colombian income from wildlife resources with the fact that biomedical investigators in the United States are the principal primate recipients, perhaps we can arrive together at a mutually illuminating realization. It is important to understand that the urgency reflected in the subject, the site, and the generous support of the conference at which this paper was delivered is necessarily a reflection of United States biomedical research priorities and not of the priority that the Colombian Government can at present reasonably afford to assign to this matter of unquestionable mutual interest and concern.

DESCRIPTION OF COLOMBIA

As further background to our discussion of the nonhuman primate populations of Colombia, it is important to consider the principal geographic
features, the rich biological diversity, and the demography of the country.
Colombia is a nation of 1,138,914 square kilometers and an estimated
22 million people (Figure 1). The vast majority of its human inhabitants
live in its three western Andes mountain chains (cordilleras) and the
large Magdalena and Cauca river valleys between these ranges as well
as in the broad northern Caribbean coastal lowlands. In demographic
terms, the remaining approximately 5 percent of the population occupies
the other two-thirds of the country, including the humid rain forests of
the Pacific coast, the broad eastern plains of the Orinoco drainage, and
the Colombian Amazon Basin. Present estimates are that nearly 60 percent of the population has an urban distribution. Population growth is
4 percent or more annually, and it is reported that 55,000 families enter
the rural population each year. Urban growth is even greater, with
approximately 100,000–200,000 people entering the work force annually.
The unemployment rate is estimated to be about 14 percent. Economists
estimate that a 7.5 percent annual increase in gross national product
(GNP) is needed to stabilize unemployment at present levels. The GNP
increase during 1971 was only about 4.5 percent.

Land presently in agricultural use throughout Colombia totals about
38.2 million hectares,* with at least 85 percent represented by livestock
grazing activity. About 64.5 million hectares are forested, and some 40
percent of this total is now being commercially exploited or studied for
future exploitation. The rest of the land area includes 3.7 million hectares
of lakes, lagoons, and rivers, 2.5 million hectares of swamps, 3 million
hectares of "paramos" (the tundralike altitudinal belt between the
timber-line and the permanent snow line), and 2 million hectares of
cities and roads.

PRIMATE DISTRIBUTION

The extent of nonhuman primate distribution throughout Colombia is
exceedingly broad. The upper altitudinal limits for some species are as
high as 3000 meters. However, the largest number of species and the
greatest populations are found nearer to sea level in the Pacific coastal

---

* A hectare is equal to 10,000 square meters.

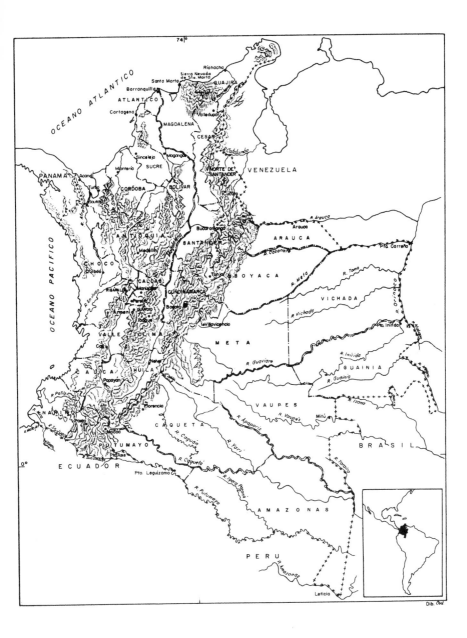

Figure 1. Colombia.

area, the Caribbean lowlands, the expansive and intermittently forested eastern plains, and the Caqueta and Putumayo river drainages of the Middle Amazon. Unfortunately, the nonhuman primate populations of Colombia and their ecological relationships are not easily assessed as are those of *Homo sapiens*.

The main centers of primate export (Cooper, 1968a; Harrisson, 1971; Middleton et al., 1972; Thorington, 1972a) are Leticia, in the Comisaria of Amazonas, and Barranquilla, on the Caribbean coast. Barranquilla draws primates principally from the northern Departments of Bolivar, Sucre, Cesar, Cordoba, and Magdalena. Some primate specimens also reach Barranquilla from points as distant as Leticia, Florencia, Puerto Leguizamo, and Puerto Asis in Amazonian Colombia, from Villavicencio and a few other localities in the eastern plains, as well as from Acandi, Sautata, and Turbo in or near the northern Department of Choco, and close to the border of Panama.

With regard to the total Colombian faunal exportation, the Amazon region yields about one-third of all live animals and two-thirds of all skins, while the proportions shipped from the Barranquilla market are just the reverse. With primates this trend does not hold, in that at least as many are currently exported from Leticia as from Barranquilla. However, in terms of resource study and management, the northern trade center is perhaps more significant, since it is known that the majority of primates exported from Leticia are not trapped in Colombia but in the not-too-distant regions of Brazil and Peru (Cooper, 1968b; Harrisson, 1971; Middleton et al., 1972). Attempts to determine the exact geographic sources and proportions of such trade in the Amazon Basin are most difficult due to the absence of any reciprocal agreements or controls for faunal exploitation among the three countries involved.

Of the primate forms exported by Colombia, squirrel monkeys (*S. sciureus*) (Figure 2), white-lipped and white-moustached marmosets (*S. nigricollis* and *S. mystax*—the latter form occurring only on the southern bank of the Amazon), hooded capuchins (*C. apella*), long-haired and black spider monkeys (*A. paniscus belzebuth, A.p. paniscus* and/or *A.p. chamek*), white-handed and dusky titis (*C. torquatus* and *C. moloch*), red uakaris (*C. rubicundus*), and saki monkeys (*P. monachus*) come from the Amazon collecting region served by Leticia. The primates collected commercially in northern Colombia include night monkeys (*A. trivirgatus*, Figure 3), cotton-topped and white-handed marmosets [*S. oedipus* (Figure 4) and *S. leucopus*], white-throated and white-fronted capuchins (*C. capucinus* and *C. albifrons*), and long-haired and brown-headed spider monkeys (*A. paniscus hybridus* and *A.p.*

Figure 2. Squirrel monkey *(Saimiri sciureus).*

robustus). Although the night monkeys and white-fronted capuchins have a broad distribution including much of the Amazon, those currently exported from Colombia are primarily collected in the northern Caribbean lowlands. At times this general picture has been confused, due to the fact that, as mentioned previously, animals from the Amazon Basin are often shipped to Barranquilla for exportation. Because of the ease of internal air transportation and the availability of inexpensive surface transportation in Colombia, it is seldom safe to assume that primates or other faunal forms have necessarily been collected near their localities of purchase or exportation.

Figure 3.   Night (or owl) monkey *(Aotus trivirgatus).*

THE HUNTING/TRAPPING OF PRIMATES

The general economic and sociologic considerations regarding wildlife exploitation in Colombia include the fact that many rather poor people living largely from day to day are involved at the most basic level, that of hunting and/or trapping. With primates as with most other exploited faunal forms, it is unlikely that primary-level collectors are individually responsible for any large numbers of animals reaching secondary or final holding compounds each week or each month. In fact, it is unlikely that the majority of animal hunters capture exclusively any particular species. The species hunted is determined more by the area in which

Figure 4.   Cotton-topped marmoset *(Saguinus oedipus).*

the hunter lives, the seasonal fluctuations of species availability and/or access, the existence of a market or buyer, and the time he has available from farming, fishing, wage labor, or other activities. Typically a hunter has learned informally something about the habits of many species in his region. When he goes hunting, it is not necessarily with a certain species in mind, but more likely with a number of possibilities determined by previous experience and the various conditions of the moment. There are, of course, some professional hunters, but these men are usually involved in exploitation of animal skins of relatively greater economic value, for example, crocodilians, the spotted cats, and river otters. But even in the hunting of animals for their skins, the supposition on the part of many observers that the trade is highly organized is fostered largely by viewing the bulging warehouses of skin dealers. In fact, such a concentration of hides usually represents the little-organized and accumulated efforts of hundreds of subsistence hunters and a large number of secondary buyers and transporters.

COMMERCIAL PRIMATE EXPLOITATION

The history of commercial primate exploitation in Colombia had its roots in happenstances as long ago as 300 to 400 years. Indians and early colonists often kept young primates as pets. The appeal of the antics of such species is practically universal, as attested by the proportions of present-day primate pet trade and the popularity of these species in zoos. It is thus not too surprising that some Colombian primates reached Europe and elsewhere in the days of sailing ships. Primate pets were then most often the result of food or sport hunting (i.e., babies and juveniles re-covered from the bodies of killed adults) and perhaps even of casual sport trapping of adults and juveniles of smaller species (e.g., marmosets) by young boys. In many respects, such methods are not too far from the state of the art today, although an increase in the pet trade has produced a shift in priorities. Therefore, the species that are most often hunted as food (*Lagothrix, Ateles, Alouatta,* and *Cebus*), and for which occasional live juveniles were once a byproduct, have in many areas (largely the Amazon Basin) come under greater pressure from the commercial value now possessed by these former byproducts.

Today, insofar as we know, the only exploitation of primates in Colom-bia that deserves the description of "organized" is that of several species which are exported largely for biomedical research use. In the Leticia area, Mike Tsalickis has developed a relatively organized collection net-work for *S. sciureus, S. nigricollis,* and *S. mystax,* as well as for a modest number of *L. lagothricha* in one small locality. In Barranquilla, Simon Daza has developed a less formal collection network for *A. trivirgatus, C. albifrons,* and *C. capucinus,* as well as for smaller numbers of *Ateles paniscus* sbspp. [All these particular primates are supplied almost exclu-sively to biomedical research through the Tarpon Zoo in Tarpon Springs, Florida (Clarkson, 1972; Cooper, 1968b; Middleton et al., 1972; More-land, 1970).] Such collection networks usually consist of a small boat or boats driven by employees who visit trappers and/or small local buyers to purchase animals and thus eliminate the need for these people to make long, hot trips into Leticia or Magangue (the latter, located near the confluence of the Cauca and Magdalena rivers, is a principal regional collection area for subsequent shipment to Barranquilla). The major effects of such networks are to communicate market demand to the trappers and local buyers and, secondarily, to safeguard the health of captive primates by removing them from often inadequate local holding compounds and transporting them in the least stressful manner to more functional facilities. In such holding facilities as those of Tsalickis and Daza, animals are kept under observation and are provided with food, water, some medication, and relatively sanitary cage conditions. The latest information on virus disease susceptibility [e.g., *Herpesvirus simplex* susceptibility of night monkeys and *H. tamarinus* susceptibility of night monkeys and marmosets (Burkholder and Soave, 1970; Clarkson, 1972; Emmons et al., 1968; Holmes et al., 1963; Hunt and Melendez, 1966; Melendez et al., 1969; Melendez et al., 1971; Melnick et al., 1964; Tate et al., 1971)] is usually applied in order to avoid potentially dangerous interspecific exposure and to limit the caging of susceptible species to small groups captured in the same locality.

It is certain that such collection networks, however informal, through minimizing morbidity and mortality after capture and by collecting only the numbers of animals needed, result in better utilization of Colombian primate resources than does the traditional high-volume, low-overhead, and less-organized exotic pet trade. The Colombian Government is aware that holding and shipping mortality, though not adequately documented, is much higher for primates and other species involved in pet-oriented commerce than it is in the research animal trade. Also, the uncontested fact that the vast majority of Colombian animals that enter the pet trade do not live even one year (and often less than one month) after reaching the importing country is a growing deterrent to the continued justification of such commerce for the relatively small amount of national and local income thus obtained.*

Because biomedical investigation requires animals in reasonably good states of health and acclimation to conditions of captivity, the price paid by the ultimate user is often 10–20 times the price paid to the original trapper. Admittedly, local politics is often played in Colombia and elsewhere with the great disparity between prices paid to the collector and those ultimately paid by a medical investigator. However, both the higher purposes being served by such specially handled and therefore

* Subsequent to the presentation of this paper, exploitation of primates in Colombia for the pet trade was prohibited; see Resolution 392, April 18, 1973, in Table 2 in the following section.

expensive animals and INDERENA'S distaste for the mechanics and ethics of the pet trade (in which all corners are cut in order to sell live animals to exotic pet fanciers for a multiple of only 3–8 times the hunter's price), dictate that closer examination of priorities and values beyond superficial questioning of price differentials be given. It is also obvious that further restriction or even elimination of primate exploitation for the exotic pet market would have the result of protecting the natural resource for use in the more humanitarian areas of basic and applied biomedical research. In return for the thoughtful consideration currently being given by Colombia to the laboratory primate requirements of research, investigators should evaluate their needs for experimental primates very critically, both in terms of the species selected and the numbers utilized.

Several examples will serve to define our concern in this area. The recent advances in malaria chemotherapy research using *Aotus trivirgatus* from Colombia's Caribbean coastal lowlands (e.g., Geiman et al., 1969; Jervis et al., 1972; Schmidt, 1971; Tsalickis, 1968; Wilson and Voller, 1972; Young, 1970) has created unprecedented exploitation of this species population. As will be discussed below, it has been difficult to study the exact effects of such research pressures on natural populations, both because of limited available human and fiscal resources and the inadequacy of present survey methods (Thorington, 1972b). Combining these facts with the continuing habitat destruction by expanding human population and the general lack of success in breeding *Aotus* in captivity, one must conclude that demands on this natural resource in northern Colombia should be minimized to protect its future availability.

Another case in point is that of the cotton-topped marmoset (*S. oedipus*), a species unlike *Aotus* in that it is endemic to a small portion of northern Colombia. Because of its beauty, its vigor, and the closeness of its habitat to the Barranquilla export market, it has long been a popular exotic pet trade item. In the early 1960s when biomedical investigators first began to take advantage of the existing pet trade in Neotropical primates to obtain promising new laboratory species, *S. oedipus* was one of those species utilized (Dreizen et al., 1971; Hampton, 1964; Skougaard, 1964). Subsequently, the Colombian Government became aware of the threatened status of this species and in 1969 prohibited its capture and trade. However, at the time of this writing, it is still exported illegally in some numbers. In addition, requests are received regularly for legal exportation to laboratories in West Germany and the United States. Although we can sympathize with investigators who do not wish to change species after accumulating a large amount of basic data and experience, we are not aware of many research uses of S. *oedipus* for which other less endangered species of *Saguinus* will not serve. Thus we encourage investigators to avoid using S. *oedipus* whenever possible and to refuse to buy illegally exported animals. In return, Colombia will continue to give very serious consideration to permit requests for studies requiring S. *oedipus* and for which other species cannot easily be substituted. It is also anticipated that within three to five years the capture of S. *oedipus* for any purpose will be totally prohibited, and thus we encourage the establishment of breeding colonies of this species to meet future research needs.

WILDLIFE MANAGEMENT AND REGULATION

At this point it will serve our purpose to review the history of wildlife management and regulation in Colombia up to the present. The first regulation of hunting of birds and mammals was decreed in 1941 by the President of Colombia at that time, Eduardo Santos. Enforcement responsibility was left with the Ministry of Agriculture, but by all accounts was not effective due to a lack of personnel and financial resources. In the same year, Colombia became a signatory nation to the Convention for the Protection of the Flora, Fauna, and Natural Scenic Beauties of the Americas sponsored by the Pan American Union. The fact that this document was ratified by the Colombian National Congress only within the past several years may serve to indicate the rather recent development in government circles of any serious awareness of the need to protect Colombia's irreplaceable natural resources.

In 1960, the Division of Hunting and Fishing was established (Decree 1710) within the Colombian Ministry of Agriculture. This agency was concerned with the management of commercial exploitation of these faunal resources and again was somewhat less effective in practice than was the intention of its founders. At about the same time, a semi-autonomous agency, the Magdalena and Sinu Valleys Corporation (CVM), patterned after the U.S. Tennessee Valley Authority, was created in the northern Caribbean lowlands. The major accomplishments of the CVM (1960–1968) were in the important areas of fisheries research and management, forestry research and exploitation, and the biological investigation and hunting regulation of crocodilians and turtles (due largely to the pioneering efforts of Federico Medem), as well as the creation of two national parks.

In 1956, 1960, and 1961 the government of the Department of Valle in the Upper Cauca Valley and the adjacent Pacific coast issued regulations for licensing hunting and establishing hunting seasons and bag limits. These regulations were inspired largely by the concern and untiring efforts of Carlos Lehmann, another internationally recognized Colombian biologist–conservationist. Today this region is largely within the jurisdiction of the Cauca Valley Corporation (CVC), a semiautonomous agency created to guide the agricultural and industrial development of the area. Rather recently, the scope of CVC responsibility has been broadened to include the management of renewable natural resources, including wildlife.

In 1966, Fernando Ruan, then Chief of the Division of Hunting and Fishing of the Ministry of Agriculture, developed a wildlife and hunting statute which unfortunately was not accepted until more recently in a revised form. The following year, pressure was exerted to reorganize the Ministry of Agriculture, and in 1968 President Carlos Lleras Restrepo established by decree law the Institute for the Development of Renewable Natural Resources (INDERENA). This semiautonomous agency was molded by moving the Division of Hunting and Fishing outside the Ministry of Agriculture and combining it with the Magdalena and Sinu Valleys Corporation. INDERENA's jurisdiction covers all of Colombia except for the Bogota plateau and an adjacent mountain valley as well as the region governed by the Cauca Valley Corporation. Today INDERENA, directed by Fernando Ruan,[*] conducts technical activities through the Divisions of Fisheries, Forestry, Watersheds, Water Management, and National Parks and Wildlife. The responsibility for biological investigation, protection, and resource management for Colombian fauna (including primates) resides within the subdivision of Wildlife Reseach. The overall task of INDERENA is planned, coordinated, and evaluated by the National Office in Bogota and directly administered and implemented through six Regional Jurisdictions. At present, INDERENA has about 2300 professional, administrative, enforcement, and labor employees throughout Colombia. The 1971 budget was in excess of US $5 million, a lesser portion of which was secured through a loan from the Agency for International Development.

In the brief 3½ years of INDERENA'S history, over 40 separate management regulations regarding Colombian wildlife have been promulgated. Table 2 presents a brief description of all Colombian faunal regulations (drawn up both before and after the establishment of INDERENA) that affect the exploitation of primate resources and are presently in force.

[*] Fernando Ruan resigned in early 1973 and was replaced by Julio Carrizosa-Umaña.

Table 2   Colombian Faunal Regulations (1941–1972)

Decree No. 459 (President Eduardo Santos, March 7, 1941)

Article 11a: establishes in all the national territory that deer and all classes of game mammals cannot be hunted for the eight months between March 1 and November 1 each year.[a] The few exceptions listed do not include any primate species.

Article 13c: establishes a minimum head and body length (skin) of 40 centimeters for capture of the red howler (*Alouatta seniculus*).

Resolution No. 0200 (Ministry of Agriculture, October 1, 1964)

Article 1: all hunting and fishing activities are forbidden in the Sierra de la Macarena National Reserve (now an 8000-square-kilometer National Park); a later resolution extends this limit to a 5-kilometer perimeter buffer zone.[b]

Resolution No. 008 (Board of External Commerce, September 3, 1968)

Article 1: forbids the exportation of faunal specimens or products for which hunting and trade restrictions exist.

Resolution No. 574 (Director of INDERENA, July 24, 1969)

Article 1: permanently forbids the hunting of *Saguinus oedipus*, due to its endangered status.

Agreement No. 20 (Board of Directors of INDERENA, November 27, 1969)

Basic Wildlife and Hunting Statute:
- distinguishes between subsistence, sport, commercial, scientific, and control hunting.
- establishes commercial hunting license requirements, including information on the specific areas and systems of hunting to be employed, the species and numbers to be collected, the identification of possible buyers, and the names of assistants. (As a practical matter, most licenses are taken out in the names of the dealers and the actual hunters are informally considered as being their assistants.)
- establishes that licenses are to be issued for one year or less; a later regulation stipulates that they expire when the designated quota of animals is filled if this occurs prior to the actual date of expiration.

[a] The rationale for selecting these particular months as a nationwide "closed season" for mammals is unknown to the present Wildlife Research staff of INDERENA.

[b] Today, hunting and fishing in National Parks, Faunistic Territories, Wildlife Sanctuaries, and officially designated Areas of General Interest (together called Reservations of the National Park System) are strictly forbidden except under special license for scientific purposes. In many cases, however, enforcement has been difficult to achieve.

Table 2   Colombian Faunal Regulations (1941–1972) (continued)

Resolution No. 531 (Director of INDERENA, July 29, 1970)

Article 1: establishes requirements for licensing private wildlife breeding farms ("zoocriaderos"), such licensing being necessary for the commercialization of production at any time of the year according to an INDERENA-approved plan of management.

Agreement No. 18 (Board of Directors of INDERENA, August 5, 1970)

Article 2: establishes a "repopulation" quota of 10 percent of the approved number of faunistic species designated in each commercial license. The stated intention was that such specimens would be supplied by license holders either through purchase from private breeding farms or from Faunistic Territories under the management of INDERENA for release (by INDERENA) in underpopulated areas under strict biological control.

Resolution No. 031 (Director of INDERENA, February 4, 1971)

Article 1: establishes the prices for purchase from INDERENA of animals from Faunistic Territories for fulfillment of the faunistic "repopulation" requirements of Agreement No. 18 of August 5, 1970. The following prices are those established for individuals of each primate species and include the cost of handling and transportation (by INDERENA) to a suitable underpopulated area for release:

	Col. $ (Columbian pesos)
Aotus trivirgatus	100
Callicebus moloch	150
Callicebus torquatus	200
Cacajao rubicundus	500
Cebus spp.	120
Saimiri sciureus	180
Lagothrix and *Ateles* spp.	800
Alouatta spp.	400
Saguinus spp. and *Cebuella*	600

Article 3: establishes that hunters will pay (at the time the license is received) the corresponding value (10 percent) of the species for which they take out licenses; this amount is equal to the established value of 10 percent of the individual specimens of each species for which the license is acquired.

Resolution No. 225 (Director of INDERENA, April 19, 1971)

Article 1: authorizes the commercial hunting of *Aotus trivirgatus* for exclusive use of biomedical investigation (malaria) for the rest of the closed season (from April 19 to October 13, 1971).

Article 2: authorizes maximum capture of 100 *Aotus* per month and a maximum total of 700 during the entire period.

Table 2   Colombian Faunal Regulations (1941–1972) (continued)

Resolution No. 002 (Director of INDERENA, January 14, 1972)

Article 1: establishes that the value of faunistic "repopulation" services rendered by INDERENA to commercial hunting licenses of the Municipality of Leticia (includes all of the Comisaria of Amazonas) will be the following (listing of primates only):

	Col. $ (Colombian pesos)
Aotus trivirgatus	4
Saimiri sciureus	4
Lagothrix lagothricha	22
Cebuella pygmaea	3
Saguinus spp.	4

Article 2: establishes that the value of faunistic repopulation service in Leticia will be paid when permits for animal shipment are issued, rather than with the issuance of a hunting license.

Article 3: establishes that in the Municipality of Leticia hunting and sale of all mammals and products will be permitted at all times of the year (with several important exceptions not including any primate species).[c]

Resolution No. 568 (Director of INDERENA, May 31, 1972)

Article 1: authorizes the commercial hunting of *A. trivirgatus, S. oedipus,* and *C. albifrons* in the Atlantic Region of *INDERENA.*

Article 2: indicates that commercial licenses will be issued during the period of June 1 to October 31, 1972, permitting the capture of a maximum of 100 *A. trivirgatus,* 25 *S. oedipus,* and 10 *C. albifrons* per month by each license holder.[d]

Resolution No. 569 (Director of INDERENA, May 31, 1972)

Article 1: authorizes lifting of the ban on commercial hunting of *S. sciureus, S. mystax, S. nigricollis,* and *C. pygmaea* from June 1 to September 30, 1972, in the region of Leticia.

Article 2: establishes a maximum capture of 60 individuals of each of the

[c] In the preamble of this resolution, it is stated that INDERENA is taking the above steps temporarily, during which time studies leading to a more adequate basis for the management, development, and commercialization of wildlife products in the zone of Leticia will be undertaken.

[d] The consideration given for this action is the importance of these species in human medical research. In accordance with Presidential Decree No. 459 of March 7, 1941, such mammals could not ordinarily be captured between March 1 and November 1.

Table 2   Colombian Faunal Regulations (1941–1972) (continued)

above species during the entire four-month period for each commercial license.[e]

Resolution No. 392 (Director of INDERENA, April 18, 1973)[f]

Article 1: as of June 1, 1973, prohibits the capture and commercialization of all nonhuman primate species in Colombia while studies are being made of their biological cycles, geographic distribution, and natural population densities.

Article 2: enables INDERENA to permit capture of nonhuman primates only when they are destined for scientific investigation or supply of museums and zoos, and then only when such exploitation will not endanger natural populations. For such purposes the Director of INDERENA will establish quotas for each species.

Article 3: provides that parties interested in obtaining commercial hunting licenses for the implementation of Article 2 must make a solicitation in writing to the Division of National Parks and Wildlife of INDERENA, indicating the destination of the primates desired and presenting certification from competent Colombian authorities that the entity desiring the primates is scientific in character or a museum or a zoo. If the request is granted, the Division will so indicate in writing to the Regional Director of INDERENA in the area of intended capture, along with any other requirements established by INDERENA.

Article 4: violations will result in confiscation of the primates involved and the maximum fine which can legally be levied.

Resolution No. 407 (Director of INDERENA, April 25, 1973)[g]

Article 1: authorizes the commercial capture of *Ateles paniscus, Aotus trivirgatus, Cebus albifrons, Cebus capucinus,* and *Saguinus oedipus* until November 30, 1973.

Article 2: establishes the following quotas for each species: *Aotus trivigatus,*

[e] The consideration given for this action is the importance of these species in human medical research. Validity of this Resolution is questionable, since Resolution No. 002 of January 14, 1972, establishes hunting of these and most other mammalian species during the entire year in the Leticia region and therefore no ban exists that must be lifted. Also *S. mystax* does not occur in Colombia.
[f] This resolution was passed after delivery of this paper and has been added here prior to submission to the publisher.
[g] This resolution was passed after delivery of this paper and has been added here prior to submission to the publisher.

2000; *Ateles paniscus,* 250; *Cebus albifrons,* 150; *Cebus capucinus,* 150; *Saguinus oedipus,* 500.

Article 3: establishes the following maximum numbers which can be captured in any one month during the period covered by this resolution: *Aotus trivirgatus,* 400; *Ateles paniscus,* 50; *Cebus albifrons,* 25; *Cebus capucinus,* 25; *Saguinus oedipus,* 100.

Article 4: provides for granting of commercial hunting licenses for this provision subject to the procedures and requirements of Resolution No. 392 of April 18, 1973.

INDERENA'S DILEMMA

The future of Colombian primate populations is officially the responsibility of the Subdivision of Wildlife Research. INDERENA's concerns and principal research and management objectives lie in two general areas. First, we are acutely aware of our relative ignorance of the ranges, population biology, and ecological determinants of most species (Hernandez-Camacho and Cooper, in press). Second, we are very conscious of the need for studies of the effects of commercial exploitation and of habitat alteration on natural primate populations of all species so affected. At present there are six INDERENA biologists working within the broad area of wildlife investigation and management who average as much as 50 percent of their time in the field. There are also nine volunteers in the Colombia-Peace Corps Environmental Program now working as INDERENA wildlife biologists. With specific regard to primate field investigations, INDERENA biologists together are able to give the approximate equivalent in effort of one full-time person. Of three primate-oriented Peace Corps volunteers now with INDERENA, two are presently spending nearly all their time in the field in relatively fixed localities in the northern Caribbean lowlands, and a third is working a majority of the time on primate-related projects in the Wildlife Research office and laboratory in Bogota. For purposes of perspective, it is perhaps important to note that, aside from those of INDERENA, all other Colombian professionals engaged in wildlife-related research (approximately 15) are associated with seven different educational institutions. With several prominent exceptions, the majority of these biologists are university professors with interests tending more toward classical taxonomy than to questions of life cycles, population ecology, and so on.

While INDERENA is concerned with the status of local populations of species such as *C. albifrons, A. paniscus, A. trivirgatus,* and, of course, with the entire population of *S. oedipus,* an objective analysis of the effort and support required to obtain the needed information is discouraging in light of the limited available human and financial resources. Also, given the great demographic pressures in most areas of present major primate exploitation and the great difficulty of regulation enforcement (related to questions of illiteracy, poverty, and cultural patterns which produce more concern for the present than for the future), it is very tempting to direct the limited financial and human resources that are at hand to other more promising areas. It will be possible to establish natural reserves to protect the existence of some threatened primate species or populations, but the future of many populations as a commercial resource is probably limited. If the problem were one created entirely by commercial exploitation, the matter would be far less complex. As it is, INDERENA is seriously considering limiting the exploitation of Colombia's remaining primate natural resources for selected purposes of biological and medical investigation.* Such regulation could be rather effective, with the cooperation of the United States and other user countries. Nevertheless, with a human population that is doubling every 20 years, it is inevitable that greater and greater reduction of nonhuman primate habitat will occur in many areas of Colombia.

On the brighter side, there still exist broad areas of Colombia which contain sizeable populations of many primates species and in which at present their commercialization seldom, if ever, occurs. These regions include most of the Pacific coast, the Upper Magdalena Valley, the Catatumbo Basin of the western Lake Maracaibo drainage, the Sierra Nevada de Santa Marta on the Caribbean coast, the majority of the broad eastern plains, and even much of the Colombian Amazon. The principal reasons that such areas remain today are the low human population levels in those areas and the great distance or inconvenience of transportation to markets. INDERENA's policy is to set aside as rapidly as possible large areas containing relatively undisturbed ecosystems of the various major Colombian biotypes. It is felt that expending the limited available human and physical resources in this way represents the most intelligent investment that can currently be made in Colombia's future. We are hopeful that at the same time this investment may also best serve to guarantee the future controlled supply of Colombian primates for important scientific investigations.

* And since this paper was presented, action has been taken, per Resolution 392, Table 2.

BREEDING PROGRAMS

The title of this book, *Primate Utilization and Conservation,* brings us finally to a consideration of possibilities other than completely natural production or Neotropical primate supply. INDERENA's interest in fostering within Colombia the development of breeding colonies of most major commercialized forms of wildlife is represented by a "zoocriadero" program currently being developed within the Wildlife Subprogram. The intents of this effort are *(1)* to do feasibility and cost analysis studies on the captive rearing of a variety of such faunal forms and *(2)* to develop a technology for producing the more promising species, which could permit private enterprise to profitably enter this field.

Some consideration has been given to including selected primate species in this program. However, considerable input from potential users of such captive-reared stock will be needed before any serious effort can be undertaken. Questions such as the principal species of interest, the quality of produced animals, and the protection of such a market from competition with wild-caught Neotropical primates from other exporting countries must be satisfactorily answered. Thorington (1969) has mentioned the likelihood that "careful management of monkey population in the wild and a systematic cropping of these populations would be more profitable and present fewer problems than the actual raising of animals in captivity." The only present experimental breeding activity of a Neotropical primate in Colombia is that of Mike Tsalickis on a 400-hectare seral forested island in the Amazon River not far from Leticia (Clarkson, 1972; Tsalickis, 1968; Tsalickis, 1972). This project was initiated in 1967 with the introduction of large numbers of mature squirrel monkeys captured in the region. Although the island was not previously inhabited by *Saimiri,* in concept and practice the project is far nearer to the management of wild populations suggested by Thorington than to a captive rearing program. A field team representing Cornell University, Harvard University, University of the Andes (Bogota), and several other interests recently (summer of 1972) completed a three-month study of the present status of the *Saimiri* population on the island, and so we can expect at least a preliminary evaluation of this project to appear in the near future.

At this time, INDERENA's interests in captive primate production are more in the area of confined or caged populations in circumstances where greater management and control can be exerted. Clearly, the basic question is one of specimen quantity versus specimen quality. If the need is simply for more specimens of certain species approximating the same quality as those captured in the natural habitat, this implies modest management intervention to maximize the production of such species in well-controlled areas of natural habitat. The costs would have to be kept extremely low and the production high to compete with "unfarmed" exports. It is also certain that in developing population densities greater than usual in nature for any given species, the risk of unplanned "discovery" of natural population regulating mechanisms must be acknowledged. Our preference for more controlled production circumstances assumes that some market exists for animals of higher quality, including known age, parentage, diet, reproductive experience, and so on. At the same time, we are aware of concerns such as recently expressed by Schmidt (1972), that: "Because of distance and impossibility of assuring complete control over many aspects of production and procurement, it would be a serious error to locate breeding resources in or adjacent to the areas from which nonhuman primates are currently withdrawn, specifically in Northern and Central South America, Central America, Africa, Southeast Asia and India." For this reason, INDERENA does not plan to undertake the development and evaluation of such a production effort without the collaboration of prospective users. At the same time, since any future commercial primate production would be financed and conducted privately rather than by INDERENA, we would also welcome prospective users to develop pilot projects (such as that of Mike Tsalickis) together with private interests in Colombia. This approach would have the supervision of INDERENA through its zoocriadero licensing program and would avoid the possible future complications of transferring INDERENA-developed primate production technology to an intending commercial producer. We believe that with close coordination of foreign users and Colombian producers, the potential problems of adequate control of production and procurement mentioned by Schmidt could be largely, if not entirely, avoided.

SUMMARY

In summary, we have attempted to indicate something of the status and problems of commercial primate exploitation and management in Colombia. This report has of necessity been couched in terms of overall wildlife resource exploitation. We have reported the species and numbers of primates legally exported from Colombia in 1970 and noted both that the total primate export value represents only 3 percent of Colombia's income from wildlife resources and that the United States is the principal primate importer. The geography, demography, and land use patterns of Colombia have been briefly described, as well as the geographic areas that supply the Leticia and Barranquilla primate exportation centers. The history of Colombian commercial primate exploitation has been reviewed, including some socioeconomic aspects and the opportunistic outlook of hunters. Some distinctions have been made between the primate supply methods of biomedical research and the exotic pet market trades. The need for cooperation of biomedical research users in the species selected and numbers of primates utilized has been noted. The history of wildlife regulation and management in Colombia has been detailed, including the formation, technical activities, and human and fiscal resources of INDERENA. All existing regulations affecting primate commerce have been outlined and the present professional resources devoted to primate biological investigation discussed. The dilemma of INDERENA with regard to protecting undisturbed populations within the present and future Reservations of the National Park System vis-à-vis dedicating current efforts to protecting populations already under heavy pressure was mentioned. Perspectives for future supply of Colombian primate species for biomedical research have been discussed, including various possibilities for developing commercial breeding programs in Colombia.

REFERENCES

Aaberg, T. M., and Machemer, R. (1970). Correlation of naturally occurring detachments with long-term retinal detachment in the owl monkey. *American Journal of Ophthamology* 69(4):640–650.

Allman, J. M., and Kaas, J. H. (1971). A representation of the visual field in the caudal third of the middle temporal gyrus of the owl monkey (*Aotus trivirgatus*). *Brain Research* 31:85–105.

Baerg, D. C., and Young, M. D. (1970). *Plasmodium falciparum* infections induced in the black spider monkey, *Ateles fusciceps*, and black howler monkey, *Alouatta villosa*. *Transactions of the Royal Society of Tropical Medicine and Hygiene* 64(1):193–194.

Bates, M. (1944). The saimiri monkey as an experimental host for the virus of yellow fever. *American Journal of Tropical Medicine* 24:83–89.

Bates, M., and Roca-Garcia, M. (1945). The douroucouli (*Aotus*) in laboratory cycles of yellow fever. *American Journal of Tropical Medicine* 25:385–389.

——— (1946). Experiments with various Colombian marsupials and primates in laboratory cycles of yellow fever. *American Journal of Tropical Medicine* 26: 437–453.

Beisher, D. E. (1968). The squirrel monkey in aerospace medical research. In L. A.

Rosenblum and R. W. Cooper (Eds.), *The squirrel monkey*. New York: Academic Press, pp. 347–364.

Burkholder, C. R., and Soave, O. A. (1970). Isolation, identification, and experimental transmission of *Herpesvirus T* from an owl monkey (*Aotus trivirgatus*). *Laboratory Animal Care* **20**(2):186–191.

Cho, C. T., Feng, K. K., Voth, D. W., and Liu, C. (1972). Experimental antiviral chemotherapy for disseminated *Herpesvirus hominis* infection in marmosets. *Pediatric Research* **6**:384 (abstract only).

Clarkson, T. B. (1972). Quarantine, conditioning, and production of nonhuman primates for scientific use in the country of origin. In *Second international symposium on health aspects of the international movement of animals* (Scientific Publication No. 235). Washington, D.C.: Pan American Health Organization, pp. 33–38.

Clarkson, T. B., Bullock, B. C., Lehner, N. D. M., and Feldner, M. A. (1968). *The squirrel monkey as a laboratory animal* (Publication 1594). Washington, D.C.: National Academy of Science, National Research Council.

Cooper, R. W. (1968a). Squirrel monkey taxonomy and supply. In L. A. Rosenblum and R. W. Cooper (Eds.), *The squirrel monkey*. New York: Academic Press, pp. 1–29.

———— (1968b). Small species of primates in biomedical research. *Laboratory Animal Care* **18**(2):267–279.

Cranmer, M., Peoples, A., and Chadwick, R. (1972). Biochemical effects of repeated administration of *p,p*-DDT on the squirrel monkey. *Toxicology and Applied Pharmacology* **21**:98–101.

Davis, N. C. (1930). Susceptibility of capuchin (*Cebus*) monkeys to yellow fever virus. *American Journal of Hygiene* **11**:321–343.

Deinhardt, F., and Deinhardt, J. (1966). The use of platyrrhine monkeys in medical research. *Some Recent Developments in Comparative Medicine: Symposia of the Zoological Society of London* **17**:127–159.

Deinhardt, F., Holmes, A. W., Capps, R. B., and Popper, H. (1967). Studies on the transmission of human viral hepatitis to marmoset monkeys. I: Transmission of disease, serial passages, and description of liver lesions. *Journal of Experimental Medicine* **125**:673–688.

Dreizen, S., Levy, B. M., and Bernick, S. (1971). Studies of the biology of the periodontium of marmosets. X: Cortisone-induced periodontal and skeletal changes in adult cotton top marmosets. *Journal of Periodontology,* **42**(4):217–224.

Emmons, R. W., Gribale, D. H., and Lennette, E. H. (1968). Natural fatal infection of an owl monkey with herpes-T virus. *Journal of Infectious Diseases* **118**:153–159.

Falk, L. A., Wolfe, L. G., and Deinhardt, F. (1971). Oncogenesis of *Herpesvirus saimiri* in marmosets. *Federation Proceedings* **30**:514.

Geiman, Q. M., Siddiqui, W. A., and Schnell, J. V. (1969). Biological basis for susceptibilty of *Aotus trivirgatus* to species of Plasmodia from man. *Military Medicine* **134**:780–786.

Gengozian, N., Batson, J. S., and Smith, T. A. (1962). *Tamarinus nigricollis* as a laboratory primate. *Proceedings of the international symposium on bone marrow therapy and chemical protection in irradiated primates.* Rijswijk, The Netherlands: Krips, pp. 245–269.

Hampton, J. K., Jr. (1964). Laboratory requirements and observations of *Oedipomidas oedipus. American Journal of Physical Anthropology* 22:239–244.

Hanson, H. M. (1968). Use of the squirrel monkey in pharmacology. In L. A. Rosenblum and R. W. Cooper (Eds.), *The squirrel monkey.* New York: Academic Press, pp. 365–392.

Harrisson, Barbara (Ed.) (1971). Conservation of nonhuman primates in 1970. *Primates in medicine,* Vol. 5. Basel: Karger, pp. 1–99.

Hernandez-Camacho, J. I., and Cooper, R. W. (in press). The nonhuman primates of Colombia. *Proceedings of the ILAR conference on the distribution and abundance of neotropical primates,* Battelle Seattle Research Center, Seattle, Washington, 1972.

Holmes, A. W., Dedmon, D. E., and Deinhardt, F. (1963). Isolation of a new herpes-like virus from South American marmosets. *Federation Proceedings* 22:334.

Holmes, A. W., Wolfe, L., Rosenblatte, H., and Deinhardt, F. (1969). Hepatitis in marmosets. Induction of disease with coded specimens from a human volunteer study. *Science* 165:816–817.

Hunt, R. D., and Melendez, L. V. (1966). Spontaneous herpes-T infection in the owl monkey (*Aotus trivirgatus*). *Pathologia Veterinaria* 3:1–26.

Hunt, R. D., Melendez, L. V., King, N. W., et al. (1970). Morphology of a disease with the features of malignant lymphoma in marmosets and owl monkeys inoculated with *Herpesvirus saimiri. Journal of the National Cancer Institute* 44: 447–465.

Hunt, R. D., Melendez, L. V., King, N. W., and Garcia, F. G. (1972). *Herpesvirus saimiri* malignant lymphoma in spider monkeys; a new susceptible host. *Journal of Medical Primatology* 1:114–128.

INDERENA (Oficina de Planeacion) (1971). *Anuario de la fauna silvestre en Colombia—1970* (mimeographed).

Jervis, H. R., Sprinz, H., Johnson, A. J., et al. (1972). Experimental infection with *Plasmodium falciparum* in *Aotus* monkeys. II: Observations on host pathology. *American Journal of Tropical Medicine and Hygiene* 21:272–281.

Katzin, D. S., Connor, J. D., Wilson, L. A., and Sexton, R. D. (1967). Experimental *Herpes simplex* infection in the owl monkey. *Proceedings of the Society for Experimental Biology and Medicine* 125:391–398.

Laemmert, H. W., Jr. (1944). Susceptibility of marmosets to different strains of yellow fever virus. *American Journal of Tropical Medicine* 24:71–81.

Levy, B. M. (1963). Induction of fibrosarcoma in the primate *Tamarinus nigricollis. Nature* 200:182–183.

———— (1971). The nonhuman primate as an analogue for the study of periodontal disease. *Journal of Dental Research* 50(2):246–253.

Levy, B. M., Taylor, A. C., Hampton, S., and Thoma, G. W. (1969). Tumors of the marmoset produced by Rous sarcoma virus. *Cancer Research* 29:2237–2248.

Lorenz, D., Barker, L., Stevens, D., et al. (1970). Hepatitis in the marmoset,

Saguinus mystax. Proceedings of the Society for Experimental Biology and Medicine **135**:348–354.

Machemer, R., and Norton, E. W. D. (1968). Experimental retinal detachment in the owl monkey. I: Methods of production and clinical picture. *American Journal of Ophthalmology* **66**:388.

Malinow, M. R., Maruffo, C. A., and Perley, A. M. (1966). Experimental atherosclerosis in squirrel monkeys (*Saimiri sciureus*). *Journal of Pathology and Bacteriology* **92**:491–510.

Mann, G. V., Andrus, S. B., McNally, A., and Stare, F. J. (1953). Experimental atherosclerosis in cebus monkeys. *Journal of Experimental Medicine* **98**:195 .

Maruffo, C. A., and Portman, O. W. (1968). Nutritional control of coronary artery atherosclerosis in the squirrel monkey. *Journal of Atherosclerosis Research* **8**:237–247.

Melendez, L. V., Daniel, M. D., and Hunt, R. D. (1970). *Herpesvirus saimiri* induced malignant lymphoma: Recovery of the viral agent from the fatally affected animals. In R. M. Dutcher (Ed.), *Comparative leukemia research 1969*. Basel: Karger, pp. 741–753.

Melendez, L. V., Espana, C. Hunt, R. D., et al. (1969). Natural *herpes simplex* infection in the owl monkey (*Aotus trivirgatus*). *Laboratory Animal Care* **19**(1):38–45.

Melendez, L. V., Hunt, R. D., Daniel, M. D., et al. (1970). Lethal reticuloproliferative disease in *Cebus albifrons* monkeys by *Herpesvirus saimiri*. *International Journal of Cancer* **6**:431–435.

———— (1971). Acute lymphocytic leukemia in owl monkeys (*Aotus trivirgatus*) inoculated with *Herpesvirus saimiri*. *Science* **171**:1161–1163.

Melendez, L. V., Hunt, R. D., Daniel, M. D., and Fraser, C. E. O. (1971). DNA viruses from South American monkeys: Their significance in the establishment of primate colonies for biomedical research. In *Defining the laboratory animal*. Washington, D.C.: National Academy of Sciences, pp. 550–563.

Melendez, L. V., Hunt, R. D., Daniel, M. D., and Trum, B. F. (1970). New World monkeys, Herpes viruses and cancer. In H. Balner and W. I. B. Beveridge (Eds.), *Symposium on infections and immunosuppression in sub-human primates*. Copenhagen: Munksgaard, pp. 111–117.

Melendez, L. V., Hunt, R. D., King, N. W., et al. (1972). *Herpesvirus ateles*, a new lymphoma virus of monkeys. *Nature New Biology* **235**(58):182–184.

Melnick, J. L., Midulla, M., Wimberly, I., et al. (1964). A new member of the herpesvirus group isolated from South American marmosets. *Journal of Immunology* **92**:596–601.

Middleton, C. C., Clarkson, T. B., Lofland, H. B., and Prichard, R. W. (1964). Atherosclerosis in the squirrel monkey. Naturally occurring lesions of the aorta and coronary arteries. *Archives of Pathology* **78**:16–23.

Middleton, C. D., Moreland, A. F., and Cooper, R. W. (1972). Problems of New World primate supply. *Laboratory Primate Newsletter* **11**(2):10–17.

Moreland, A. F. (1970). Nutritional status and problems of feeding newly imported primates. In R. S. Harris (Ed.), *Feeding and nutrition of nonhuman primates*. New York–London: Academic Press, pp. 24–43.

Nahmias, A. J., London, W. T., Catalano, L. W., et al. (1971). Genital *Herpesvirus hominis* Type 2 infection: An experimental model in *Cebus* monkeys. *Science* 171:297–298.

Osuga, T., and Portman, O. W. (1971). Experimental formation of gall stones in the squirrel monkey. *Proceedings of the Society for Experimental Biology and Medicine* 136:722–726.

Paradiso, J. L., and Fisher, R. D. (1972). *Mammals imported into the United States in 1970.* (Special Scientific Report—Wildlife No. 161, U.S. Department of Interior). Washington, D.C.: Government Printing Office.

Portman, O. W., and Andrus, S. B. (1965). Comparative evaluation of three species of New World monkeys for studies of dietary factors, tissue lipids, and atherogenesis. *Journal of Nutrition* 87:429.

Rabin, H., and Cooper, R. W. (1971). Tumor production in squirrel monkeys (*Saimiri sciureus*) by Rous sarcoma virus. *Laboratory Animal Science* 21(5): 705–711.

Roca-Garcia, M., and Sanmartin-Barberi, C. (1957). The isolation of encephalomyocarditis virus from *Aotus* monkeys. *American Journal of Tropical Medicine and Hygiene* 6:840–852.

Ranney, R. R., and Zander, H. A. (1970). Allergic periodontal disease in sensitized squirrel monkeys. *Journal of Periodontology* 41:12–21.

Scherer, W. F., Breakenridge, F. A., and Dickerman, R. W. (1972). Cross-protection studies and search for subclinical disease in New World monkeys with different immunologic types of dengue viruses. *American Journal of Epidemiology* 95: 67–79.

Schmidt, L. H. (1971). Malaria chemotherapy: An interview with L. H. Schmidt. *Bulletin-Southern Research Institute* 24(1):3–14.

——— (1972). Problems and opportunities in breeding primates. In W. I. B. Beveridge (Ed.), *Breeding primates.* Basel: Karger, pp. 1–22.

Skougaard, M. R. (1964). Distribution kinetics of tritiated thymidine in marmosets. *Acta Odontologica Scandinavica* 22:693–743.

Sobel, H., Mondon, C. E., and Means, C. V. (1960). Pigmy marmoset as an experimental animal. *Science* 132:415–416.

Stare, F. J., Andrus, S. B., and Portman, O. W. (1962). Primates in medical research with special reference to New World monkeys. In D. E. Pickering (Ed.), *Research with primates.* Beaverton, Oregon: Tektronix Foundation, pp. 59–66.

Tate, C. L., Lewes, J. C., Huxsoll, D. L., and Hildebrandt, P. K. (1971). *Herpesvirus T* as the cause of encephalitis in an owl monkey (*Aotus trivirgatus*). *Laboratory Animal Science* 21(5):743–745.

Thielen, G. M., Gould, D., Fowler, M., et al. (1971). C-type virus in tumor tissue of a woolly monkey (*Lagothrix* spp.) with fibrosarcoma. *Journal of the National Cancer Institute* 47:881–889.

Thorington, R. W., Jr. (1969). The study and conservation of New World monkeys. *Anais de Academia Brasileira de Ciencias* 41(supl.):253–260.

——— (1972a). Importation, breeding, and mortality of New World primates in the United States. *International zoo yearbook,* Vol. 12. London: Zoological Society of London, pp. 18–23.

———— (1972b). Censusing wild populations of South American monkeys. In *Second international symposium on health aspects of the international movement of animals.* (Scientific Publications No. 235). Washington, D.C.: Pan American Health Organization, pp. 26–32.

Tsalickis, M. (1968). Letters: More on Amazonian fauna. *Science* 162:1432.

———— (1972). *Trapping, husbandry and transport conditions of South American primates destined for research,* Vol. 12. London: Zoological Society of London, pp. 23–26.

Voller, A., Richards, W. H. G., Hawkey, C. M., et al. (1969). Human malaria (*Plasmodium falciparum*) in owl monkeys (*Aotus trivirgatus*). *Journal of Tropical Medicine and Hygiene* 72:153–160.

Wellde, Bruce T., Johnson, A. J., Williams, J. S, et al. (1971). Hematologic, biochemical, and parasitologic parameters of the night monkey (*Aotus trivirgatus*). *Laboratory Animal Science* 21(4):575–580.

Wilson, R. J. M., and Voller, A. (1972). Comparison of malarial antigens from human and *Aotus* monkey blood infected with *Plasmodium falciparum. Parasitology* 64:191.

Wissler, R. W., Frazier, L. E., Hughes, R. H., and Rasmussen, R. A. (1962). Atherogenesis in the cebus monkey. I: A comparison of three food fats under controlled dietary conditions. *Archives of Pathology* 74:312.

Wolfe, L. G., Deinhardt, F., Theilen, G. H., et al. (1971). Induction of tumors in marmoset monkeys by Simian Sarcoma Virus, Type 1. (*Lagothrix*): A preliminary report. *Journal of the National Cancer Institute* 47:1115–1120.

Wolfe, L. G., Falk, L. A., and Deinhardt, F. (1971). Oncogenicity of *Herpesvirus saimiri* in marmoset monkeys. *Journal of the National Cancer Institute* 47:1145–1162.

Young, M. D. (1970). Busqueda de un modelo experimental para paludismo humano. *Reportes Medicos* 1(4):39–40.

CHAPTER 7

J. Stephen Gartlan

THE AFRICAN COASTAL RAIN FOREST AND ITS PRIMATES— THREATENED RESOURCES*

INTRODUCTION

The coastal forest blocks of West and Central Africa are located between latitudes 10°N to 5°S and extend from Sierra Leone to the mouth of the Congo (Zaire) River. They rarely reach more than 300 miles (480 kilometers) inland, except where they merge with the vast Congo Basin Forest.

The coastal forest strip is divided into two blocks of unequal size by a tongue of dry country, the Dahomey Gap, which reaches down from the northern savannas to the coast. Following Moreau's (1963) classification, the area to the west of the Dahomey is referred to here as Upper Guinea, and that to the east and south as Lower Guinea. The Lower Guinea Forests can be divided into three distinct areas. The largest of them is the extensive lowland forest of the Congo Basin, which, during the Pliocene, was submerged in a huge lake. The other two, which formed unsubmerged refuge areas during the Pliocene, include a western strip of forest along the Atlantic coast between the Cross River and the Congo River (the Cameroon–Congo Coastal Strip, or CCCS) and an

* The field work reported here was supported by British Medical Research Council Grant G. 969/524 B.

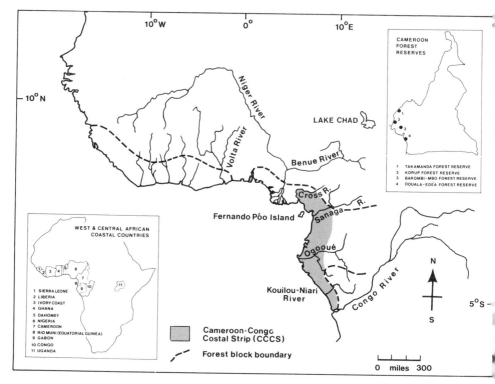

Figure 1.   The coastal forest areas of West and Central Africa.

area that formed the eastern rim of the Pliocene Lake in what is now eastern Zaire and Uganda. This paper is chiefly concerned with the Atlantic coastal forest strip (CCCS) and particularly that part of it which lies in Cameroon (Figure 1). The whole area of this forest is 150 by 750 miles (240 by 1200 kilometers), and it is characterized botanically by an abundance of *Lophira alata* and *Sacoglottis gabonensis* (Letouzey, 1968).

The CCCS is an archaic forest having affinities both with the forests of Upper Guinea and with those of South America. It is very well endowed with endemic species of flora and fauna, and is one of the richest areas of the world for primates. It holds clues to the theory of continental drift, to patterns of climatic change in past eras, and to the evolution, diversification, and radiation of the primates. It is therefore an area of extraordinary scientific interest.

THE FLORA OF UPPER AND LOWER GUINEA AND
THEIR AFFINITIES

The forests of Upper and Lower Guinea differ in wealth of their flora. White (1962), in a study of speciation and geographic variation in *Diospyros* (Ebenaceae), found only 4 endemic species in the forests of Upper Guinea, compared with 24 in the forests of Lower Guinea. This difference cannot be explained merely by the larger area of the Lower Guinea forests, for 22 of the 24 species found there occur in the CCCS. The total area of this strip is much less than that of the Upper Guinea forests and represents only a fraction of the total Lower Guinea block.

Faron (1968) described a similar situation in his study of the Ochnaceae, the CCCS being much richer in species than the Upper Guinea forests.

There is evidence (Richards, 1963) that the eastern portions of the Upper Guinea forests, that is, the parts lying now in Ghana and the eastern Ivory Coast, may be relatively recent, and that during past periods of arid climate this area may have been invaded by savanna. On the other hand, the western portion of the Upper Guinea forests in Sierra Leone, Liberia, and western Ivory Coast was probably not as severely affected by the change in climate and may have acted as a refuge area for forest species. The existence of vicarious species of flora and fauna in the two areas tends to confirm this.

Voorhoeve (1965), in a study of the high forest trees of Liberia, noted that many of the species were more closely related to those of the CCCS than to those of the adjacent forests of the Ivory Coast and Ghana. He remarks especially on the high number of vicarious species in the family of Caesalpiniaceae.

In addition to affinities between the flora and fauna of the CCCS and those of the western part of the Upper Guinea forests, which are indicative of continuity prior to the period(s) of desiccation, the forests of the coastal strip, and particularly those of the CCCS, show evidence of an even more ancient continuity with the rain forests of South America.

Letouzey (1968), in an intensive botanical study of the forests of Cameroon, points out that the genera *Stigmaphyllon* and *Heteropteris* of the family Malpighiaceae are widely distributed in tropical America, whereas in Africa they are confined to the west coast. *Stigmaphyllon* has 60 species in Central America and the Antilles and only a single species (*S. oratum*) in Africa. *Heteropteris* has 80 tropical American species, as compared with a single one of the West African coast. The genus

Octhocosmus has about eight species in tropical America, whereas only two occur in Africa and one of them, *O. chippii*, is exclusively coastal.

Even more striking is the evidence afforded by the Vochysiaceae. This family has five tropical American genera, but in Africa is represented only by the monospecific *Erismadelphus exsul*, whose distribution is restricted to the coastal forests of Southeast Nigeria and Cameroon. There it occurs in company with the more common and widely distributed *Sacoglottis gabonensis* (Humiriaceae), which itself belongs to a genus that is an important constituent of the tropical American rain forest.

The presence in West African tropical forests of a small group of unique species belonging to genera that are widespread and have undergone much adaptive radiation in tropical America leads to the conclusion that the African species are relics that have maintained themselves in an area of relatively stable climatic and ecological conditions, where they have been subjected to little selective pressure.

THE PRIMATE FAUNA OF UPPER AND LOWER GUINEA AND THEIR AFFINITIES, WITH SPECIAL REFERENCES TO THE CCCS

The relative numbers of endemic primate species in the Upper and Lower Guinea forests show a similar pattern (Table 1) to that of the

Table 1. *Endemic Primate Species of Upper Guinea and Those of Lower Guinea Occurring in the CCCS*

Upper Guinea	CCCS of Lower Guinea
Procolobus verus	*Arctocebus calabarensis*
Cercopithecus campbelli	*Galago alleni*
Cercopithecus petaurista	*Euoticus elegantulus*
Cercopithecus diana	*Colobus satanas*
Cercocebus atys	*Cercopithecus pogonias*
Colobus polykomos	*Cercopithecus cephus*
	Cercopithecus lhoesti preussi
	Miopithecus talapoin
	Cercocebus torquatus
	Papio leucophaeus
	Papio sphinx
	Gorilla gorilla

flora. The forests of the CCCS support a remarkably rich and diverse primate fauna, there being 12 endemics as compared to 6 in Upper Guinea.

The wealth and diversity of the CCCS forest primate fauna are well illustrated in the block between the Cross and the Sanaga rivers (excluding the island of Fernando Póo) which covers an area of approximately 100 by 150 miles (160 by 240 kilometers). This small forest supports isolated populations of *Cercopithecus lhoesti* (which does not occur again until the eastern Zaire/Uganda refuge area), of *Colobus badius,* and of *Gorilla gorilla* (Figure 2). It represents almost the entire range of *Papio leucophaeus* (Figure 3), *Cercopithecus erythrotis camerunensis,*

Figure 2.   *Gorilla gorilla gorilla.*

Figure 3. *Papio leucophaeus.*

C. pogonias pogonias, and *C. nictitans martini,* and also harbours *Arctocebus calabarensis, Galago alleni, Euoticus elegantulus, Galagoides demidovii, Cercopithecus mona, C. aethiops, Cercocebus torquatus,* and *Pan troglodytes.*

Among the primate fauna there are few clear-cut examples of vicarious species. This may be partly a reflection of the present confused state of primate taxonomy, which might be clarified if methods could be used to separate closely allied allopatric pairs. Examples of vicarious primate species in the Upper and Lower Guinea forests are *Cercopithecus nictitans stampflii,* which is restricted to Liberia and the western edges of the Ivory Coast, and *C. nictitans martini,* which occurs in the CCCS. Here, the relationship between them is so close that Hayman (1940) considers them to be synonymous. Again, in the red Colobus group, whose taxonomy is particularly confused, *C. badius preussi*, the CCCS representative, is considered by Elliot (1913) to be vicarious with *C. b. ferrugineus* (=*C. b. badius*), whose distribution extends from eastern Sierra Leone and Liberia into the western part of the Ivory Coast.

The coastal forest blocks of West–Central Africa are divided into smaller units by rivers which run more or less at right angles to the coast. Major rivers which act as barriers within the CCCS are the Cross, the Sanaga, the Ogooué, and the Kouilou-Niari. Of these, it is the Sanaga that constitutes the main faunal barrier. This river divides *Cercopithecus n. nictitans* living on the south bank from *C. n. martini* on the north bank, and *C. pogonias grayi* from *C. p. pogonias*, and probably *Papio sphinx* from *P. leucophaeus* (contrary to popular belief; e.g., Dandelot, 1968). *Cercopithecus neglectus* does not cross the Sanaga to the north bank, nor does *Colobus satanas*. Similarly, *Cercopithecus lhoesti* is not found south of the river. These differences between the primate fauna of the south and north banks are strikingly apparent near the mouth of the Sanaga, in the Douala-Edéa Reserve.

Within a forest block such as that between the Cross and Sanaga Rivers are many different local habitats which are colonized by different primate species. Thus, *Miopithecus talapoin* is essentially a species of riverine forests within the rain forest belt. *Cercopithecus lhoesti* is primarily a montane forest species, and *C. neglectus* is characteristic of swamp forests. *Colobus badius* inhabits high, primary forest, whereas *Cercopithecus mona* thrives in secondary and mangrove forests. As these various habitats are liable to different exploitation pressures, so the species inhabiting them are also differentially susceptible. For example, the high forests inhabited by *Colobus badius* and *Colobus satanas* hold much commercially attractive timber, and if the primary trees are cut down, these populations may well become extinct. On the other hand, the extensive cutting of primary forests has already led to large-scale replacement by secondary growth and, as a result, *Cercopithecus mona*, which is able to colonize this habitat, appears to be extending its range.

PRESSURES ON THE PRIMATE FAUNA

Destruction of the Forest Habitat

It is known that the flora and fauna of a particular region form an interacting dynamic ecosystem. Interference with one will inevitably affect the other.

In Cameroon, the timber from the coastal forests of the CCCS has been exploited for domestic consumption over many years, and since the beginning of the century, European colonists have been exporting hardwood logs to Europe.

By 1961, exploitation of the southeastern Cameroon forests for commercial timber led to the exportation of 400,000 cubic meters of timber in a single year (Letouzey, 1968). This figure represents the felling of approximately 60,000 trees of 50 centimeters or more in diameter near the base.

Exploitation of the southwest forests on a large scale began only in 1958, reaching a peak in 1960–61 when approximately 150,000 cubic meters of logs were exported, representing about 21,000 trees of 50 centimeters or more in diameter. The industry then declined temporarily, but in recent years (1971 and 1972) it has increased spectacularly. Much forest rich in obeche (*Triplochiton scleroxylon*) was completely felled.

Recently, there has been a dramatic increase in the number of applications for timber concessions in the southwest Cameroon forests, which is apparently related to the advent of timber companies from the Ivory Coast, where the forests have been more or less completely worked out. Whereas in the late 1960s only 2 companies were operating in the southwest Cameroon forests, there are now 12. Production of logs in this area in 1972–73 will almost certainly be a record and is expected to continue at a high rate. The concessionary areas of primary forest are now almost all allocated to various timber companies and many of them have already been completely felled.

Primates and their habitats will be severely affected by the immediate felling, but this is not all, for the secondary results of timber exploitation also have various and profound effects upon them. The majority of commercially desirable trees are high-forest or emergent types. Obeche (*Triplochiton scleroxylon*), for example, may reach 160 feet or more, with a crown 60 feet in diameter and 40 feet deep. When such a tree is felled, it brings down with it many other trees and lianes, devastating a wide area. The destruction thus caused by the felling of 81,000 such trees throughout the Cameroon forests, as in 1960–61, can well be imagined.

Furthermore, to obtain access to remote forests, timber exploitation companies construct roads. These roads open the area, and people then move in to settle, bringing with them shifting cultivation. Subsistence crops such as plantains, yams, and cocoyams are planted, often after the felling and clearing of an area of forest by slash-and-burn techniques. Cash crops such as cacao, coffee, and bananas are also planted, necessitating the clearance of even larger areas of forest. The normal cycle of regeneration of the timbered forest is thus retarded or more often completely inhibited. Such exploitation roads also allow ready access for hunters, who, with modern weapons, are able to make serious inroads into primate populations.

Reforestation programs are at present rudimentary. It takes approximately 80 years for a mature forest to regenerate, even if it is left undisturbed after timbering. But neither the timber companies nor the governmental forest services seem prepared to take such a long-term view of reforestation. As a result the logging trade is simply living off the capital of the forest. Seldom is there any attempt to reconstruct the former species composition of the forest, and if reforestation is done, usually monospecific stands are planted. Exotic species are often introduced, such as *Eucalyptus* and the fast-growing softwood *Gmelina arborea*; or, if indigenous species are used, they are confined to fast-growing softwoods such as *Pycnanthus angolensis* or *Terminalia superba*, or to commercially desirable hardwoods such as mahogany, *Entandophragma* spp. It is extremely unlikely that homogenous stands of this type will be able to support the rich primate fauna that exists in the mixed forests.

The overall effects of timbering are thus the destruction of the natural habitat of most forest primates and production of conditions favorable to the invasion of destructive human beings. The scale of this process is already causing serious concern for the preservation of the primates.

Persecution By Man

The human invasion of the African lowland rain forests probably began not more than 1000 years ago (Murdock, 1959). It probably had little effect on the indigenous Cameroon flora and fauna until about 100 years ago. When human hunting pressures were limited to bow-and-arrow techniques (as is still the case today in many areas of Zaire) and when traps had to be constructed from lianes rather than from metal wire, there was probably little adverse effect on the primate population of the forest. The situation changed dramatically with the advent of firearms and of freely available wire for the construction of efficient and relatively permanent traps. There seems to have been little tradition of bow-and-arrow hunting in the forests of Cameroon (although this was apparently practiced in Rio Muni), and before the advent of firearms human hunting was probably restricted to trapping.

The effect of these changing pressures, particularly the advent of fire-arms, is evident in the case of *Colobus badius preussi*. Specimens of this species were collected from the forest of Barombi Mbo in Cameroon in the last decade of the nineteenth century. This species has not been found in that forest for at least the last 25 years, and probably consider-ably longer, and the last surviving population is now located about 90 kilometers (56 miles) to the northwest, in the remote Korup Reserve. This example illustrates the need for protected reserves if such unique species are to be saved from extinction.

Colobus badius has an alarm and defense system which has been evolved in response to avian predation by such species as the crowned hawk-eagle, *Stephanoëtus coronatus*. *Colobus badius* is a high-forest species which feeds on the leaves at the top of the canopy. When alarmed, it climbs to the top of the tree it is in and sits there immobile. It may give screeching alarm calls, but other group members do not respond to these in any marked degree. Remaining immobile at the top of the forest canopy may be an adequate defense against eagles or against hunters equipped with bows and arrows, but it is completely inadequate against a double-barreled shotgun: they are thus easy and vulnerable targets.

Similarly, the habits of *Papio leucophaeus* render it especially liable to modern methods of human predation. Gartlan (1970) described how small, one-male subunits of *P. leucophaeus* congregate into large, multi-male hordes. These aggregations are characterized by various loud vocal-izations, the deep roaring calls of the adult males and the shrill, penetrat-ing trills of the juveniles. They are therefore easily located by the hunter. Contemporary hunters generally make use of small packs of dogs. The response of *P. leucophaeus* when confronted by a dog is to climb up out of reach, often into quite small saplings. From here they are easily picked off by the hunter, and 20 or more may be shot in a single encounter. The present level of predation is almost certainly too high to be sustained by such a geographically restricted species without seriously affecting its chances of survival.

Although most predation of primates is accomplished by means of firearms, trapping does account for some. In Southwest Cameroon, Rio Muni, and Gabon, noose traps are set along poles in order to catch *Miopithecus talapoin*. Occasionally, *Papio leucophaeus*, *Cercocebus torquatus*, *Cercopithecus mona*, and *C. lhoesti* are also trapped in wire noose traps on the ground. In Rio Muni, gorillas were often caught in robust traps constructed in the same way. Live primates which are offered for sale by hunters are generally those that have been trapped, and often the wound caused by the wire noose is still visible on the wrist or ankle. Otherwise they are young animals that have been caught after the mother has been shot. However, the numbers taken alive and for which a purchaser can be found represent only a very small minority of the total captured. The great majority die or are killed and are then used for domestic consumption.

The primate species that feature most prominently in the export trade, and which are well-known in the laboratories and primate centers of the United States and Europe, are the wide-spread savanna species—the long-tailed baboons (*Papio* spp.), *Cercopithecus aethiops*, and *Erythrocebus patas*. All three are present in Cameroon, and certainly neither *C. aethiops* nor the savanna baboons are as yet threatened by the export trade, provided that any increase is associated with a carefully controlled cropping program. *Erythrocebus patas* is rather a special case. It has a more limited distribution than the other two species (Figure 4) and also lives in ecologically more critical zones. Struhsaker and Gartlan (1970) showed that one of the major features of the ecology of *E. patas* was its dependence on water holes toward the end of the dry season. Any delay in the onset of the rains, which is quite common in the sahel savanna regions, could therefore affect its local status adversely. There is thus a greater need for any cropping of this species to be carefully controlled. Fortunately when there is international trade, there is the prospect of mutually agreed controls, both in the country of origin and in the country of import, governing any species that becomes endangered.

Up to now, the forest primate species of the CCCS have not been used to any significant extent in the primate export trade. Recently, however, there has been a demand for *Miopithecus talapoin* as a laboratory animal. The forest primates, having a more limited distribution than the savanna ones, are *ipso facto* much more vulnerable. *Papio leucophaeus*, for example, is found only in a very small forest area between the Cross and Sanaga rivers, whereas the savanna baboons range from East to West Africa and as far south as the southernmost tip of the continent. In contrast to the savannas, the habitats of the forest primates in developing countries contain economic resources of great value. Whereas the savanna vegetation remains little disturbed, the forests are being destroyed by felling. The Muslim peoples of the northern savannas generally do not hunt monkeys for food, whereas in the forest zone, monkeys are a preferred food of the populace and are hunted and trapped relentlessly. Except for chimpanzees, the forest primates have not yet featured significantly in the export trade and the depradation of their numbers has not been for this purpose. The greatest drain by far has been the

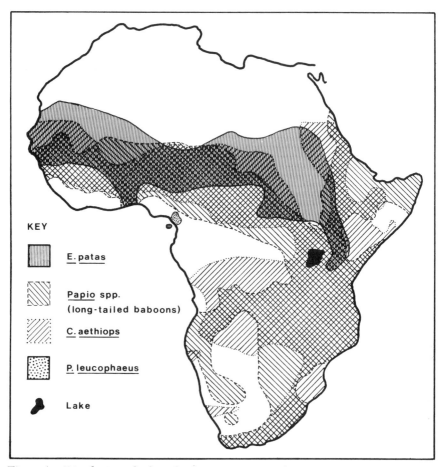

KEY

E. patas

Papio spp.
(long-tailed baboons)

C. aethiops

P. leucophaeus

Lake

Figure 4.   Distribution of selected primate species in Africa.

numbers killed for food and this predation is still increasing. For these reasons, the forest primates are currently greatly at risk and their preservation can only be achieved by national and international measures of conservation and by international agreements on their import and export.

CONCLUSIONS AND RECOMMENDATIONS

It is clear that exploitation of the flora of the West African coastal forests is inevitable. The high forest trees are a major economic resource for the developing countries of the CCCS. The best that can be hoped for is that the timber will be cropped in a systematic and efficient manner, with a minimum of incidental damage, that there will be an adequate reforestation program, and that some areas will be left untouched.

The primate fauna itself should be regarded as a valuable national resource, but from lack of appreciation and adequate surveillance it is one that is being rapidly depleted both by activities that are legal, such as timbering and the clearing of land for plantations, and by illegal hunting and trapping in forest reserves.

Damage to the fauna of a primary forest where timber felling takes place can be minimized but cannot be entirely prevented. Felling upsets delicate ecological balances; food trees are removed and the normal cycle of regeneration is disturbed. Therefore, to save the forest primates from extinction and to retain parts of the CCCS as relatively untouched ecosystems, properly supervised forest reserves will have to be set up. All exploitation of flora and fauna in these reserves will have to be prevented. This will demand stringent and early action by the governments of the countries concerned, as well as adequate financial assistance, perhaps from outside bodies interested in conservation, so as to permit adequate policing of the reserves.

Within the CCCS there are areas that are unattractive to the timber companies, because they are too remote, because the terrain is too difficult for timber-extracting vehicles, or because they are relatively poor in commercially attractive trees. Such areas in Cameroon include the Takamanda Reserve, which has an isolated population of gorillas; the Korup Reserve, with its isolated population of *Colobus badius*; and the Douala-Edéa Reserve, which straddles the faunal barrier of the Sanaga River and includes a viable population of the rare black Colobus (*C. satanas*). Fortunately it seems likely that the Korup and Douala-Edéa Reserves will shortly be declared National Parks in Cameroon. Korup, which comprises approximately 125,000 hectares,* extends from 5°25′N to 4°54′N and from 8°42′E to 9°5′E. It contains at least 13 primate species. Douala-Edéa, which comprises about 150,000 hectares, extends from 3°15′N to 3°52′N and from 9°32′E to 10°4′E and contains at least 15 primate species and subspecies.

If and when they are completely protected against human exploitation, these forest reserves will be unique in Africa. The natural heritage of the country will be maintained instead of being destroyed by ruthless

---

* A hectare is a unit of area in the metric system equal to 10,000 square meters or 2.471 acres.

Richards, P. W. (1963). Ecological notes on West African vegetation. II: Lowland forest of the Southern Bakundu Forest Reserve. *Journal of Ecology* **51**:123–129.

Struhsaker, T. T., and Gartlan, J. S. (1970). Observations on the behaviour and ecology of the patas monkey (*Erythrocebus patas*) in the Waza Reserve, Cameroon. *Journal of the Zoological Society of London* **161**:49–63.

Voorhoeve, A. G. (1965). *Liberian high forest trees*. Wageningen, Holland: Centre for Agricultural Publications and Documentation.

White, F. (1962). Geographic variation and speciation in Africa with particular reference to *Diospyros*. In David Nichols (Ed.), *Taxonomy and geography*, Vol. 4. London: Systematics Assn., pp. 71–103.

CHAPTER 8

Francis C. Cadigan, Jr.
Lim Boo Liat

THE FUTURE OF SOUTHEAST ASIAN NONHUMAN PRIMATES*

Since there are very few data on the amount of nonhuman primates in Laos, Vietnam, or Cambodia, we shall deal principally with Malaysia and Thailand. Our quantitative studies are almost entirely from Malaysia (Southwick and Cadigan, 1972). There is, of course, no total census from any of these countries. It is almost impossible to get a proper census of humans in most countries and certainly much more difficult to do so with monkeys and apes. One can, however, evaluate the type of habitat in which the primates live, the prevalence of suitable habitats, and the approximate group size. Similarly, one can make some estimate of the accessibility of animals to hunters. Accessibility refers to the legal restrictions (and the degree to which they can be enforced), the physical restrictions of distance and means of transport, and the (human) social restrictions arising from custom or religion.

As in every area of commerce, supply and demand plays a large part in the price, and in the case of scarce and desired animals it plays a larger part than the real cost of procurement and shipping. Thus an animal such as the orang-utan commands an exorbitantly high price in

* The research for and preparation of this paper was supported by Research Grant DADA17-72-G-9350 from U.S. Army Medical Research and Development Command, Washington, D.C.

The studies of Southwick and Cadigan (1972) in Malaysia showed a mean group size of 24 animals per group in *M. fascicularis*, of which 50 percent were adults. Since 17 percent were infants, or a rough ratio of 1 infant to 3 adults, there is a fair crop available if we can estimate that the average life span of these animals is 10–15 years. However, it will still take many groups to produce 10,000 animals for export. Even if one took all the infants and all the juveniles, it would require 833 troops each year to provide that number. Since sufficient numbers of animals must be left to maintain sizes of groups, obviously more than 833 troops would be needed on a continuing basis.

Nevertheless, the future of the long-tailed macaques looks good. These animals are found most frequently at the edge of the forest and seem to do best in secondary growth with its rich diversity of flora. In our opinion, the size of bands appears to be limited not so much by predation as by availability of food and the ability of the group to maintain visual contact. Thus, troops that live in parks or on the seashore tend to be much larger than those that live in the forest. The largest aggregate we have seen, and one that leads to very interesting speculations on the ways of raising them in semicaptivity for research purposes, is in Lopburi in Central Thailand. This group lives in the area of a small ruined temple in the center of town having a roughly circular shape with a diameter of about 100 yards. There are a few large trees and several small buildings in this area. The animals are considered as belonging to the Buddha, since they live in the temple area, and thus people gain religious merit by feeding them. Thus, there is constant (and excessive) provisioning of these animals. Virtually all adult monkeys in this group are obese, with heavy jowls and pendulous rolls of fat. In a sense, the population is "fat" also, since there were well over 100 monkeys in this area by our count.

The pig-tailed monkey (*M. nemestrina*) is in slightly greater danger, since although groups of this animal in Malaysia are usually of larger size than those of *M. fascicularis*, it is much less commonly seen at the fringe of the forest and is more likely to be found in deep forest. If, as it appears, this animal does not do as well in fringe forest, then as development of land increases, the number of pig-tailed monkeys may drop sharply. Our knowledge of its habitat preference in Malaysia is based on our casual (i.e., not systematic) observations and on the knowledge of the aborigines who hunt them for food. These animals are also taken in large numbers for export and a very few for local research work. These are the animals that are trained to pick coconuts.

The stump-tailed or red-faced macaque (*M. speciosa*) is found chiefly in Thailand, with only a slight incursion into northern Malaya (Lim, 1969). These animals are very scarce compared to the other macaques of Southeast Asia, and although in our experience they are slightly more tractable in the laboratory than other macaques, they ought not be used for research purposes if other, more common, species will serve.

The leaf monkeys of Southeast Asia constitute an interesting group (Figure 2). Except for *Presbytis entellus*, few leaf monkeys have been used in biomedical research, and except for studies of plague, little has been done with *P. entellus.* Our group became interested in the potential

Figure 2.   Dusky leaf monkey *(Presbytis obscurus).*

There is still argument raging as to whether tree shrews are primates or not. While we have our own personal bias, we are not expert enough in such things to make a pronouncement that will generate more argument. The important thing to us is that tree shrews have at least enough primate characteristics that an argument is possible. Thus, it seems to us that investigations should be made to determine in what fields of study the tree shrew could replace higher primates. The *Tupaia glis* has been colonized at the SEATO Medical Research Laboratories in Bangkok and also at other laboratories. (See Chapter 12 for a discussion of this species.) It has a high reproductive potential, is cheap to maintain, and is easy to feed. Other species have been kept in captivity, but as far as we know no one has tried to produce them in large number. Since it is known that at least one species, *T. glis*, can be produced in adequate numbers, the next steps are to determine the suitability of various species as substitutes for higher primates and, having identified a desirable candidate, to attempt colonization.

RECOMMENDATIONS

There are several situations in which monkeys live in semicaptive conditions which bring to mind possible ways to reduce the predation of man on "wild" troops. We have mentioned previously the situation in the temple at Lopburi, Thailand, for long-tailed macaques (*M. fascicularis*).

The big question, of course, is what is the future of supply of nonhuman primates from this area. For the supply of animals, specifically the silvered leaf monkey, for scrub typhus research, one could depend upon establishing an "island-type" situation analogous to the Kuala Selangor (Southwick and Cadigan, 1972) or Lima Belas (Cadigan and Lim, in press) situation, in which relatively large numbers of animals are raised in a small area. For example, at Kuala Selangor in an area of about 100 acres of which much less than half is covered by trees, there are three troops of *P. cristatus* totaling over 100 animals. The approximate density is at least 3 per acre. Such areas, whose primary use is not monkey production, could conceivably satisfy small needs but could never satisfy the large demand that we have cited previously for *M. fascicularis*. On the other hand, perhaps the rubber or oil palm planter, who sees "the monkey" as a demon out of hell that has no other thought in mind "than wanton destruction" since the young trees "have not usually been attacked as a food source" (as a planter in Malaysia was quoted in the "Straits Times"), might be led *not* to believe that "sustained control by shooting appears to be the only satisfactory solution to the problem" (also from the same quote), but rather to see them as a second crop on his land to be sold off to trappers. We realize that this may greatly disturb the ardent conservationist, but submit that it is an improvement on the current situation in which the planter shoots monkeys on the estates and the commercial supplier traps monkeys in the forests.

Another situation that might be explored is the "development" of forest areas (if rape constitutes development) in which the primates will not survive once the habitat is destroyed. Perhaps the trappers could be encouraged to hunt out those areas prior to or during their development. These areas could then be supplemented by animals raised on "islands" of forest. I would like to mention that there is no reason why only a single species should be maintained in such a situation. In situations such as Lima Belas Estate and the Penang Waterfall Gardens (Bernstein, 1967; Southwick and Cadigan, 1972), multiple species of primates are present in a noncompetitive situation. Chivers (in press) has commented that gibbons tend to be in the tops of trees and siamang slightly lower down. At Kuala Selangor, the *P. cristatus* and *M. fascicularis* have been seen intermingled while feeding. *Presbytis obscurus* and *P. melalophos* are frequently seen together. These diurnal animals in no way interfere with the nocturnal lorises.

Most important, perhaps, is to think of ways to require less than 10,000 monkeys from Malaysia. Better maintenance after capture, and improved shipping, caging, and feeding will reduce the wastage. These will come only when all those concerned realize that while "a rose is a rose is a rose," "a monkey is not a monkey is not a monkey." Each species, certainly each genus, has its own minimal requirement for survival and its optimal requirement as well. What is of trivial importance to one may be critical to another. For example, a perch in the cage is of little significance to a primarily terrestrial animal like *M. mulatta*, but it appears to be of critical importance to *P. cristatus*, an arboreal monkey. In addition, if one observes *P. cristatus* in the wild, one immediately notes that almost all these animals have their long tails hanging straight down below them. In fact, since they often sit in clusters, the easiest way to count them is by the number of tails. If this animal is put into a cage lacking space for the tail to hang down, it is analogous to putting a man into a cage that requires his neck to be kept flexed—a situation not directly incompatible with life, but one that can create a severe and cumulative

CHAPTER 9

Barbara Harrisson

CURRENT EFFORTS IN PRIMATE CONSERVATION: THE IUCN

This seminar discusses current techniques, ideas, and information leading to new concepts of primate production. The aims are to ensure the continuity of the resource and its harvest potential and to improve the quality of harvests in accordance with modern needs. The focus is mainly on primate forms that currently support the advancement of biological and medical research and industry.

The majority of these are the least vulnerable, from a conservation point of view. Rhesus and some other macaques, baboons, vervets, and squirrel monkeys have wide distributions. Their capabilities to adapt to pressures of harvesting have been demonstrated. They are traded in substantial numbers from resource countries at prices well below those of captive-bred specimens. While their natural populations may sharply decline in the future (owing to factors outside the control of research and industry in developed nations), captive breeding of them in large numbers is possible. The techniques are understood. The production of quality specimens to fulfill current and projected needs is an economic rather than a research problem.

The concern of the writer is not directly with primate production. It is with the preservation of the whole spectrum of extant primate species and of their habitats, to ensure the continuity of their natural potential for posterity. The focus is mainly on primate forms known to be threatened at this time and on others, the status of which is unknown, doubtful,

are available, but their supporting institutions are unlikely to produce grants for them unless a long-term research interest or a particular user responsibility regarding the species or area to be investigated is established. The IUCN and conservation agencies can provide support for professionals, but only if a proposed project concentrates on basic data and conservation needs rather than on detailed or long-term research interests. Since professional research careers are tied to research institutions, conservation interests are downgraded. The result is that fieldwork is mainly conducted in areas and regarding species that are relatively known and secure.

IUCN needs funds to support the maintenance and security of habitats, but the commitment of institutions and industries with an interest in primates does not normally include the habitats of these primates. An extension of their commitment becomes possible only after meeting their primary concern for captive maintenance and production in environments that they control.

This division of interest has involved IUCN with problems outside its expertise and commitment: reviews of detailed research and numerous requests to underwrite the procurement of threatened species for captive propagation. The dialogue has produced understanding, but has not improved individual or mutual capacities to protect and preserve endangered primates and their habitats.

The need for progress in this area of concern is indicated, as the deterioration of primate habitat accelerates. Best opportunities for action exist with respect to areas and species where the priorities of research and conservation coincide. Some of these have been identified in the Latin American sector, where research and industry have acquired substantial interests in species the captive propagation of which is not established or difficult (*Aotus, Ateles*), and in Southeast Asia where a damaging effect on gibbons is indicated, unless current methods of procurement and marketing become carefully controlled. These are only examples, and IUCN has often been asked to develop a list that identifies species primarily endangered by biological and medical research and industry. This list is difficult to produce, likely to be outdated at the time of publication, and likely to raise controversy and doubt. A list of species *not* endangered by current methods of harvesting and marketing, recommending them for usage, may produce better response. Species *not* included in such a list—because methods of harvesting are unknown or because captive propagation presents difficulties—should be recommended only to users who are able and ready to make a substantial commitment for the preservation of these species and of their habitats.

SUMMARY AND CONCLUSIONS

It is crucial to preserve the habitat of vulnerable primate species before human pressures become overwhelming. One way to promote preservation is by upgrading existing parks and preserves; another is to press for new parks wherever this is possible and before other human interests become imbedded.

Our weakness in conservation is partly due to lack of communication. For example, in tropical forests, the specialist advice of primatologists and ecologists could be invaluable to timber companies and could produce long-term planning in reserves, thus serving exploitation, research, and conservation interests simultaneously. The lack of dialogue with those involved in highway construction, oil, and mineral exploitation similarly applies.

IUCN and other conservation agencies have promoted a package treaty that protects vulnerable wild animals and plants as they move through the international trade. This treaty is well supported in the United States, but in the Common Market of Europe and other countries, where import and transit regulations do not take account of the conservation needs of exporting nations or are easily circumvented, it requires pressure for acceptance.

Demands and devices that promote rational usage of primate resources result in economy and create awareness in the users themselves. The development of understanding and support cannot be produced by conservationists alone. The formation of parks, the motion of legislation, and improved wildlife management require the support of scientists and interest groups. The user of primate resources must become convinced that it is up to him to take the necessary steps to ensure that these resources survive.

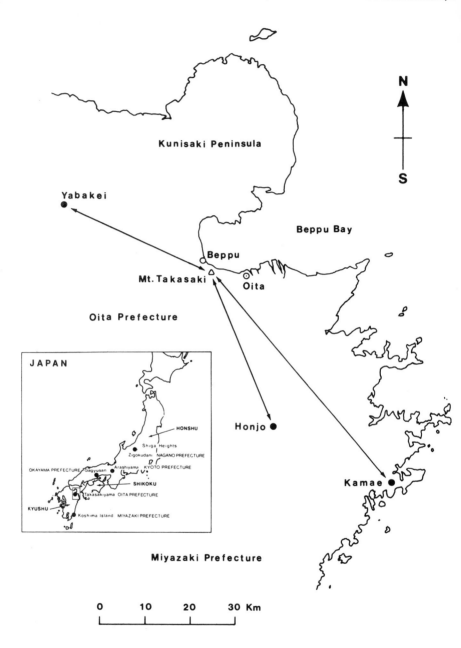

Figure 1.   Mount Takasaki and surrounding area.

with hamlets and farms. From the beginning, I could see that the monkey population on the mountain finds itself in a state of relative solitude. For it is a long way from the ranges of its closest neighboring monkey troops—Yabakei, 40 kilometers to the northwest; Kamae, 60 kilometers to the southeast; and Honjo, 40 kilometers to the southeast.

The fact that these monkeys have been able to exist on a mountain so close to two major cities is not without reasons. In the first place, because the mountain is steep, the generations of people down through the ages have stayed away from it. And second, on the slope facing the sea, nature, well protected since time immemorial, provided the monkeys with an ideal habitat. Even today, this side of the mountain up to 350 meters above sea level is rich in broad-leafed, evergreen trees. Beyond that elevation, deciduous trees abound. In sharp contrast, the slopes facing the west and south are covered only with underbrush, a telltale result of indiscriminate felling of trees that took place a long time ago. Back in 1950, the nomad range of these monkeys measured only about 5 square kilometers on the north and east slopes (Figure 2).

In August 1952, we succeeded in "provisioning" the monkeys on Koshima Island in the neighboring prefecture of Miyazaki. In November of the same year, Takasaki monkeys were also successfully provisioned, thanks to great efforts made by Oita Mayor Tamotsu Ueda and by Shinno Ohonishi, a Buddhist priest at a Zen temple at the foot of the mountain. In 1953, Mount Takasaki, as a Japanese monkey habitat, was designated by the Japanese government as a "natural monument." At the same time the mountain was designated as a national park called Mount Takasaki National Park. In March 1953, a feeding ground was created in the Zen temple compound, and the city of Oita took charge of running the park (Figure 3). At that point, the work process for us as monkey watchers underwent a drastic change. Until then, to observe the wild monkeys we always had to follow them deep into the mountain forest. This was no longer necessary. In the park, we were even able to begin to identify individual monkeys as they turned up at the feeding ground. We were able to watch over them all at close range as long as we wished. This paper is a summary of what we have observed in the past 20 years. It also summarizes actualities of that population at present.

SOCIAL CHANGES IN THE MOUNT TAKASAKI TROOP

In 1950, when I started the first phase of observation, monkeys on Mount Takasaki all belonged to one troop (Itani, 1954). In 1959, however, we

crowded neighborhood of the feeding ground. Finally, it settled down on the western slope, away from the ranges of the other three troops (Toyoshima, 1968). Eventually this troop had to be captured and removed from the mountain for several reasons. For one thing, it was damaging the agricultural produce of neighboring farms. In addition, the merit of "artificial elimination" had been gaining momentum in discussions then taking place regarding what should be done to cope with the increasing Mount Takasaki monkey population.

The monkey population on Mount Takasaki today numbers about 1400 individuals and consists of Troops A, B, and C. These three troops coexist with each other in their respective nomadic ranges situated around the communal feeding ground. The locations of the ranges are shown in Figure 4, and how the three troops used the feeding ground for the month of June 1972 is indicated in Figure 5.

POPULATION DYNAMICS

In October 1950, I saw a line of monkeys cross a ravine on the mountain and placed my estimate of its size at about 175 monkeys. In the spring of 1953, I similarly observed a group of them moving in one line and estimated the size of the group at 220 monkeys. By then, even though we had been able to individually identify many adult males and females of the group, it still was impossible to list all the individual members of the group. Therefore, the 1953 figure of about 220 for the size of the original troop before the breeding season became the basis for all the censuses we have subsequently conducted over the years for these monkeys. Each year the newborns have been added to this basic figure. But of course it was always difficult to know exactly how many died or dropped off from the troop.

In December 1962, a comprehensive investigation* was conducted, which included a reappraisal of population figures. For this census, a marking method was adopted: each monkey was given a paint marking, and the age, sex, and other features were noted. The method provided generally satisfactory results, but we discovered that the size of the group was far smaller than we had anticipated—by as many as 150. On the basis of these findings, we had to readjust our population estimates for the past (Itani et al., 1964). For the 1967 census, the same marking method involving the use of paint was employed; but we had come to realize that there were limits to the effectiveness of this marking method.

---

* Other aspects of this investigation are discussed in later sections of this paper.

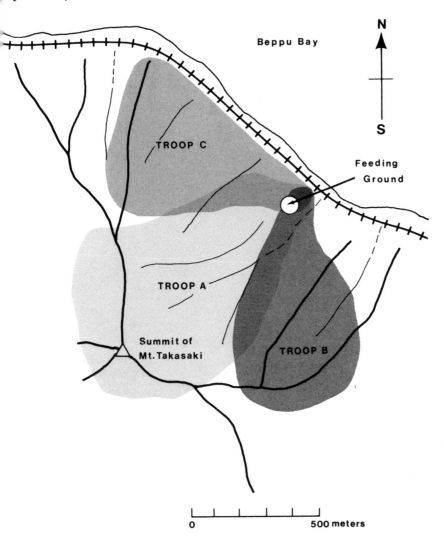

Figure 4.   Nomadic Ranges of three monkey troops on Mount Takasaki in 1972.

Table 1.   *Comparison of Status of 44 Individual Males*
in December 1962 and January 1972[a]

Name of Individual Male	Rank in 1955	Status in December 1962		Status in January 1972	
Jupiter	1	D	(Jan. 1961)		
Titan	2	A-1		S	(May 1964)
Pan	3	S	(April 1956)		
Monk	4	S	(July 1956)		
Bacchus	5	A-2		S	(May 1967)
Boor	6	A-3		S	(Aug. 1968)
Achilles	7	A-5		S	(Nov. 1964)
Dandy	8	A-6		S	(Dec. 1969)
Yubi	9	A-7		S	(Aug. 1964)
Uzen	10	S	(Sept. 1960)		
Kuro	11	A-4		S	(Feb. 1963)
Sharaku	12	D	(April 1959)		
Utamaro	13	S	(March 1960)		
Aome	14	A-10		S	(Dec. 1970)
Saruta	15	A-8		S	(Nov. 1970)
Cyrano	16	A-9		S	(June 1967)
Soba	17	S	(1956)		
Gon	18	S	(1962)		
Gen	19	S	(1955)		
Sibu	20	S	(1962)		
Pac	21	S	(1955)		
Don	22	S	(1956)		
Shiro	23	S	(1959)		

December 1962 and July 1972 of those 44 males whom I individually identified and named in 1955. Only two of the 44 were still with Troop A in 1972.

A population of Japanese monkeys not so completely isolated from others as that of Mount Takasaki will normally have a male input from another population (or populations) to balance its male output. However, in the case of the Takasaki population, the male output is overabundant in proportion. Norikoshi (in preparation) says that male monkeys begin leaving their original troops at age 3, and that by age 11 all males will have completed the process of leaving their original troops for others. Nishida (1966) notes that the process of male departure from original troops reaches its apex among 7-year-olds. A particular troop's male departure rate varies from year to year. In the case of the Takasaki

Table 1 (continued)

Name of Individual Male	Rank in 1955	Status in December 1962		Status in January 1972	
Hoshi	24	S	(1959)		
Curi	25	S	(1959)		
Akutare	26	S	(July 1958)		
Tamo	27	A-22		S	(?)
Zin	28	S	(1959)		
Pong	29	S	(1961)		
Nula	30	A-31		A-7	
Tion	31	S	(1955)		
Kin	32	S	(1955)		
Oro	33	A-11		S	(Feb. 1963)
Goemon	34	A-23		S	(Jan. 1963)
Ali	35	S	(1956)		
Gata	36	A-12		S	(Jan. 1963)
Jose	37	A		S	(Feb. 1968)
Los	38	S	(?)		
Peke	39	A-29		S	(Dec. 1970)
Toku	40	A-13		A-1	
Ika	41	A-26		S	(Feb. 1968)
Tanc	42	A-34		S	(1971)
Idi	43	S	(?)		
Bob	44	S	(1955)		

[a] D: died: A-number: male's dominance rank order in Troop A; S: seceded from Troop A.

population, an especially high number of males left their original troops in 1955 and 1956 and between 1962 and 1965. Kawanaka (in press) extensively interviewed people in an area that separates the populations of Takasaki, Yabakei, and Honjo from each other—an area that is not inhabited by monkeys—and learned that the area is almost incessantly traversed by solitary males that register varying degrees of familiarity with humans. It's safe to believe, therefore, that once on the move when leaving one troop for another, a male easily covers a distance of 40 kilometers or even more.

One thing seems evident: a male monkey on the move would find it convenient to discover another troop close by. Indeed, on Mount Takasaki, ever since the population split up into the three troops, many males have simply switched from one of the troops to another on the mountain. And there have been instances in which a male, having left its original troop, rejoins it some years later. But the number of such cases is low. Therefore, we could probably say that in leaving its original troop, the male achieves and perhaps finalizes social isolation from its relatives, particularly from its mother and sisters, and thus reduces the chance of performing incest. (This pattern of exogamy is the same with both the *Papio* and other *Macaca*. Therefore, we must not forget to bring two or more troops together, in the interest of this basic aspect of their social organization, when developing a fresh breeding colony.)

In its total size or strength, the typical Japanese monkey troop seldom exceeds 200 individuals. [For example, a troop in Gagyuzan, Okayama Prefecture, experienced five cases of fission in a span of 10 years. But due to the frequency of fission, the size of any of the troops never exceeded 200 (Furuya, 1968, 1969).] The Mount Takasaki monkeys are the sole exception. When we first observed fission to occur in that troop, the population was already over 600 monkeys. This clearly is due to the special characteristics of the terrain and to the particular location of the feeding ground. Another possible factor was the exceedingly high degree of discipline maintained in the troop by the most dominant of leaders, Jupiter, from the time of provisioning until his death in 1961.

Table 2 shows the social composition of Troops A, B, and C for the months of December 1962 and January 1972. The table data emphasize one notable point: that the trigger for fission in the original group took the form of males dropping off from the troop. One consequence is inevitable. In a newly formed troop, adult males outnumber adult females. But the ratio becomes reversed after a few years, adult females then outnumbering their male counterparts, and the troop becomes stabilized. In the case of the Mount Takasaki monkeys, fission gets under way when

Table 2   Comparison of the Social Composition of Troops A, B, and C in 1962 and 1972

	Troop A		Troop B		Troop C	
	1962	1972	1962	1972	1962	1972
Adult males	71	90	32	40	17	40
Adult females	123	280	23	65	11	75
Juveniles, 3–4 years old	86	135	45	55	19	40
Juveniles, 1–2 years old	159	250	34	60	16	60
Infants	78	135	16	40	10	35
Total	517	890	150	260	73	250

the main troop's "socionomic sex ratio" (Carpenter, 1942a) exceeds 1:2, and the ratio serves to indicate the stability of the main troop's social composition.

Among adult males belonging to the same troop, a notably stable case of "linear dominance rank order" makes itself felt, and social relations among the males seem adjusted in the light of this ranking. This ranking appears to make it possible for them to coexist. Between 1953 and 1956 (Itani, 1954), there were classes clearly differentiated by age group among males, but as the population grew, this differentiation became blurred. In the beginning of our study, by the same token, the pattern clearly indicated that the center of a troop is comprised of dominant males, females, and juveniles, and that young adult males are on the fringes. But this social structure, too, has declined in clarity.

Nevertheless, the status of the most dominant male remains stable. Troop A is a case in point. Even though this troop now numbers 890 monkeys, its leadership and integration are being perfectly maintained. In turn, since 1953, Jupiter, Titan, Bacchus (Figure 7), Boor, and Dandy have taken over as the most dominant male leader, a position now as-

Figure 7.   Bacchus and his followers.

Table 3   Succession of the Most Dominant Males in Troop A and the Periods of Dominance

Dominant Male	Period of Dominance	Length of Dominance
Jupiter	1953–January 1961	More than 8 years
Titan	January 1961–May 1964	3 years, 4 months
Bacchus	May 1964–May 1967	3 years
Boor	May 1967–August 1968	1 year, 3 months
Dandy	August 1968–December 1969	1 year, 4 months
Toku	December 1969–to present	2 years, 7 months

sumed by the sixth-generation leader, Toku (Table 3). The succession of leadership through the generations has generally been carried out smoothly. Each time, it followed the death of a leader or his departure from the troop. It has not touched off any social disturbance in the troop (Mizuhara, 1971). The genealogy of five of the leaders from Jupiter to Dandy is not clear. Clear, however, is the case of Toku, who was born to the troop that he now leads (Figure 8). He has never left his troop and assumed his status as its leader in 1969. Toku is not unique in this aspect, for we have observed other males who, without ever dropping off from

Figure 8.   Titan (left, rear) and Toku (right).

the troop to which they were born, have assumed important roles in it. But there is a far greater number of males who, as we have discussed above, drop off from their native troops and join others. What causes some males to leave their troop and others to remain has never been clear. The manners of grouping within a troop also differ from one generation to another, depending on the leader's personality, the pattern of nomadism, and the kind of relationship that exists among member monkeys. For example, Figure 9 shows the various ways in which the

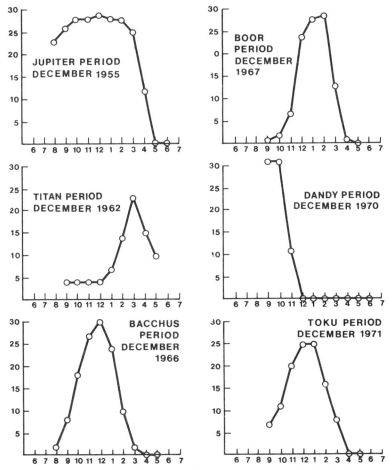

Figure 9.   Comparison of feeding ground use patterns in each leadership period of Troop A.

main troop has used the feeding ground during different periods of leadership.

Female Japanese monkeys do not leave their original troops unless they are involved in the process of fission. In other words, Japanese monkey troops are basically different in social composition from species such as *Indri, Tarsius, Callicebus,* and *Hylobates* that persist in providing the basis of social units in pairs of a male and a female each (Itani, 1972). With all the latter types, both females and males have no choice but to leave the group to which they were born by the time they attain sexual maturity. In contrast, female Japanese monkeys continue to maintain kinship relations with their mothers and sisters even when advanced in age; they even form small groups within a troop based on the strength of bondage provided by blood relation. They are dependent on each other, and their mutually dependent state of affairs is their most important social relationship. Studies of any single female and her pattern of behavior will reveal one thing for certain—that the range of her most stable social contacts is confined to her own relatives, even though she may live in a troop with many members. Grooming among females belonging to different genealogical groups commonly entails greeting and appeasing behavior (Mori, in preparation). Koyama (1970) says that fission in the Arashiyama troop in fact took the form of seven of the genealogical groups separating from the nine others in the troop. He also states that ranking is clear among different genealogical groups. But such ranking among females, or ranking among genealogical groups, is not clearly defined in large troops, like those on Mount Takasaki. At least it is not as clear as that seen among males.

The mating season for Japanese monkeys also differs slightly from one troop to another for reasons that are still unknown. With the Takasaki population, it occurs late. It extends from December to April, and the breeding season is from May to September. At the time of this writing in 1972, there was one baby born in April in each of the three troops. This was followed by a total of 36 births in May and 95 in June. By the end of September, there will be about 250 newly born monkeys recorded for Mount Takasaki this year. Sexual relationship for monkeys in Japan is the same as that reported for the rhesus monkeys of Santiago Island by Carpenter (1942a and 1942b): consort relationship is achieved by a female in heat with a male, and this relationship begins to rotate in the troop. And even during the mating season, the troops' basic pattern of nomadic life and social organization is maintained.

The outlines of the three troops are clearly defined; they seldom meet with each other. Each of the monkeys is certain to which of the troops it belongs and, for that matter, to which troops other monkeys belong.

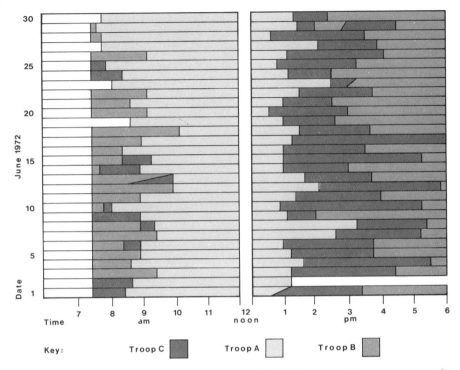

Figure 10. Daily times of the three troops at the feeding ground over a one-month period.

On the whole, it can be said that rivalry exists among the troops. When a portion of one troop comes in contact with that of another, troubles have been known to ensue. But this does not lead to overall conflict among rival troops. Today, Troop A is dominant, followed by Troop C. Troop B is subordinate to the two other troops, and this is acknowledged by all three troops. Customarily, the subordinate troop avoids coming in contact with either of the dominant troops. Then again, the dominant troop does not monopolize the feeding ground all day long. Figure 10 indicates how well the three troops stagger their feeding times.

Concerning the basic social organization of the troops, I do not think there has been any major change over the past 20 years.

CHANGES CAUSED BY PROVISIONING AND HUMAN CONTACT

If foods provided by their human guardians have resulted in elevating the monkeys' birth rate, the rate of increase has not yet been established.

But as I have pointed out earlier, without the benefit of provisioning it would have been impossible for such a large population to exist on Mount Takasaki. In addition, provisioning clearly is one reason behind the fact that no fission occurred before the population exceeded the level of 600. Takasaki, to be sure, is a small mountain. And already in 1950, substantial crop damage was reported to have been caused by monkeys at the foot of the mountain. If no provisioning had been undertaken, monkeys on Mount Takasaki could have long ago been classified by the government as harmful animals and therefore eliminated. And, in fact, provisioning has resulted in intensifying crop damage to farms immediately adjacent to the feeding ground. But because provisioning has attenuated the nomadic range of these monkeys, the overall amount of farm acreage damage has decreased. Also, crop damage has continued to decline because the municipal government of Oita, as owner of the park, has been purchasing land where the damage has been the most serious, and electric fences have been put up to prevent monkeys from wandering out of the park.

The primary influence of provisioning has been the change it has caused in the monkeys' attitude toward human beings. Back in 1955, monkeys registered a high degree of wariness toward humans. Since then, their degree of familiarity with people has rapidly climbed. This is pronounced with those monkeys of the younger generations, particularly those born after provisioning succeeded in the park. To them, humans apparently are simply part of their living environment, and many of them are not at all wary of us. But they will not forego their traditional nomadic range. At least half of each daytime period, Troop A stays in the woods to feed on natural foods. Similarly, Troop B can be found in the forest opposite the ravine in the southeast. Nomadic life clearly helps enhance troop integration and dependence on the troop on the part of member monkeys. It also obviously helps to relay wildlife routines to posterity.

Another change induced by contact with humans concerns foods and diet. In the feeding ground up until recently, sweet potatoes, soy beans, wheat, tangerines, ground nuts, apples, and the like had been provided. At present, however, the park authorities provide the monkeys with only three kinds of food: sweet potatoes, soy beans, and wheat. Ground nuts are sold to park visitors at the concession stands. Of all these items of food listed here, the monkeys had been known to eat only sweet potatoes and wheat before provisioning was started. They have developed a taste for the rest of the foods only after coming into contact with humans. The speed at which these monkeys came to accept the "new" foods was not exactly fast (Itani, 1958). Today, however, no matter what the park authorities do, the monkeys continue to expand their dietary repertoire. Covered already are all items of food sold at the concession stands, including fruit juice and even ice cream. The habit of washing sweet potatoes before eating them, a behavior first noticed among monkeys on Koshima Island, is not notable with Takasaki monkeys; there is no beach. Nor are there abundant supplies of water on the mountain to help spread the habit of washing sweet potatoes.

Still another change similarly induced is the habit of snapping at humans. Such incidents were almost nonexistent for four or five years after the start of provisioning. As the degree of familiarity with humans rose, so did the frequency of physical contact with them. Yoshiba (1965) analyzed the biting cases: 26 percent of the cases involved visitors who were bitten by monkeys for handing ground nuts to them too abruptly, and 11 percent were visitors who had gone too close to baby monkeys to suit the mothers and gotten bitten by them. A breakdown of the human victims reveals that females outnumbered males, and women in their 20s were peculiarly numerous among the victims. This seems to indicate that in our patterns of behavior and posture, there may be elements that cause monkeys to snap at us.

Around 1965, the biting incidents reached an unpleasant apex. In consequence, many of the monkeys blacklisted by the park authorities were captured and removed from mount Takasaki. The park authorities tried to do away with the bad habit by using whipping as a means of punishment. Such measures will not help reduce these incidents. The important thing for the park authorities to do is to continue to urge visitors to refrain from giving foods directly to monkeys or touching them. And this soon became clear enough on Mount Takasaki. Biting incidents began to drop sharply beginning in 1970.

ECOLOGY AND CONTROL

In studying ecological aspects of these monkeys, we have mainly been doing two things. First, we have been reporting all the results of our studies to the municipal office at Oita, which is administrator of the park. Second, we have been representing the side of the monkeys on Mount Takasaki in any discussions taking place about their relations with human communities. Over the years, new generations of researchers have been making Mount Takasaki their main field of studies. I would have to be regarded as a member of the first generation. Then came Hiroki Mizuhara, Yukimaru Sugiyama, and Kenji Yoshiba. And now there are Akisato Nishimura and Kenichi Masui. In 1965, C. R. Carpenter visited Japan for a month's research on Mount Takasaki. Later, he submitted to the park authorities his comments on ecological control of the monkey population. He said that the value of the park, which is without parallel elsewhere, should be highly appreciated. He also pointed out some of the important problems centering around the monkeys' contact with human communities and the efforts that could be taken for the purpose of maintaining their undomesticated original conditions. Finally, Carpenter elaborated on his point about how it is important to maintain a park like this one as-a place for social education.

I would not say that there have not been differences of opinion between researchers and the park authorities. We researchers are not completely satisfied with the way the park has been administered. Instead, we have stressed the importance of undertaking a number of projects, like the more thorough protection of forests as a place for the monkeys to continue their vitally important nomadic life, continued studies of vegetation as a means of making such a protection more effective, and the construction of a small museum as a depository and a place for display of research material we have accumulated. We have at the same time expressed our view of the need for maintaining an adequate distance between monkeys and humans in the park. But we have conceded at the same time that in spite of all the series of trials and errors, collaboration between us and the park authorities has made it possible to protect the Mount Takasaki monkey population for a long time. All this has been written up in a series of 12 articles by Mizuhara which appeared in *Yaen* (1964–1970).

At the present time, we are jointly developing an intensive three-year research project with the Oita municipal government. In this project we propose to concentrate primarily on the analysis of the Mount Takasaki monkey population's social composition and changes induced in the conditions of vegetation by the monkeys themselves. In 1974, we plan to offer a projection of the future population and to spell out the basic ways and means of protecting it.

The protected area of the Mount Takasaki National Park covers 330 hectares.* The feeding ground occupies 0.55 hectare. The park currently employs 24 persons, excluding its parking lot attendants. The breakdown is as follows: six clerical workers, five feeding specialists, seven guards, and six janitors. Annually, visitors to the park total somewhere

---

* A hectare is a unit of area in the metric system equaling 10,000 square meters or 2.471 acres.

between 1,750,000 and 1,800,000. Mainly, they are tourists on a visit to the neighboring hot spring resort city of Beppu and primary and junior high school pupils on their school excursion tours. The admission charge, that once was 50 yen per adult, has been raised to 100 yen (or approximately one-third of a United States dollar) in July 1972. Proceeds cover various expenditures: feed, personnel salaries, park ground and facilities maintenance, building a parking lot, and damage caused by monkeys to crops and buildings in the park's neighborhood. The daily supplies of feed consist of 400 kilograms of sweet potatoes, 18 kilograms of soy beans, and 100 kilograms of wheat.

Health examinations have been conducted on several occasions among Mount Takasaki monkeys to check for bacteria, viruses, and internal parasites. The first examination was conducted in 1961 by H. Mizuhara, S. Hayama, and M. Kaji (1962), after having captured 32 of the monkeys for the purpose. The examination was general and covered whatever check or test was possible in a short time. In addition, blood, feces, and tuberculin reaction tests were conducted. Before they were released, each of the examined monkeys was given a tattoo marking on the face for identification. Forty-eight hours later, the results of the tuberculin tests were available and all proved negative. The results of the health tests also proved normal. Internal parasite tests indicated that among the 32 monkeys, 28 carried eggs of one to four kinds. Blood (virus) tests were conducted with 29 of the captured monkeys, and the results were negative for all monkeys on adenovirus and influenza type A2 virus antibodies. Only one of the 29 was found to be carrying polio virus antibody. Thus, it was clear that for all their close contact with human beings, Mount Takasaki monkeys on the whole proved healthy.

In December 1962, a far more extensive health examination was conducted in marking the tenth anniversary of provisioning (Itani et al., 1964). The investigation covered ecology, sociology, psychology, anthropology, medical sciences, plant ecology, and other fields of science. For this purpose, a total of 56 monkeys were captured. A summary of part of the results of the medical examination follows.

Study of their mouths showed that there were few decayed teeth. Diseases within their mouths were rare. Conditions in their mouths, in other words, were good. The results of clinical tests on health and nutrition conditions were also good. Tuberculin reaction tests were conducted with all 56 captured monkeys. Only one female registered a quasipositive reaction; this female registered a positive reaction to a tubercular serum test. Feces from 49 of the monkeys were tested, and the samples proved negative on dysentery and salmonella bacteria. On parasites in the digestive system, 29 of 30 samples carried more than one kind of egg—a test result close to that produced by the previous health examination. Virus antibody tests, conducted with 47 of the captured monkeys, produced only one positive result. On influenza type A2, all of them proved negative, and on influenza type B, only one was positive. Tests on various types of polio viruses were conducted with 44 of the monkeys and all proved negative. All also proved negative on B-virus antibody. Thus it became clear that Takasaki monkeys were far healthier than their caged counterparts elsewhere. Health and medical examinations have since been conducted occasionally, but to date, there have been no results produced that might indicate the possibility of mutual contagion through contact with humans. Nor have there been any indications that might create any serious doubts about the way the population is maintained on the mountain.

Finally, a remark must be made on the subject of deformity. There was no instance of deformity seen in the population when provisioning was started. A case of deformity was first witnessed in or around 1954 (Itani and Mizuhara, 1958), and the incidence has since been on the increase. Deformity has been seen in the extremities of limbs. In the less serious cases, fingers are seen joined together. In the more serious cases, fingers or even some of the limbs are missing. With some monkeys, deformity has been seen in all four limbs. In 1954 and 1963, a monkey was seen that lacked all its limbs. Deformities like this have not been confined to Mount Takasaki monkeys; they have also been seen among monkeys at Takahashi, Okayama Prefecture, and Zigokudani, Nagano Prefecture. One thing is common with all of them: the incidence of deformity shot up after the start of provisioning.

The cause or causes have not been established for these cases of deformity. Theories have been advanced that the foods provided might have something to do with it, or the pesticides attached to foods caused it, or even that the tendency for incestuous mating might have caused it. A 1962 survey showed that eight instances of deformed monkeys existed among the population of 775, and that these cases were confined to those monkeys born after 1955. The incidence of deformity increased later. In 1970, the ratio of deformed monkeys amounted to as much as 10 percent of all those born in that year. In 1971, the ratio dropped to 5 percent. For 1972, of the 135 monkeys born so far, there were only three suffering from one form of deformity or another. The trend is that deformity is on the decline. On Mount Takasaki, there have been no special steps taken for removing deformed monkeys.

JAPANESE MONKEYS AND MOUNT TAKASAKI

In Japan there are currently no less than 30 feeding grounds for wild monkeys throughout the country. At most of these places, provisioning for wild monkeys has been carried out and/or captured monkeys are allowed to roam at will. In the main, these parks are being operated by tourism interests. Among them are some that are suffering from mismanagement. Some of the others have been forced to close down because monkeys had to be captured for causing serious cases of crop damage. Still others are confronted with the growing crop damage question, even though they remain open to visitors. It must be noted, however, that the individual *raison d'être* for many of the most noteworthy parks or feeding grounds is becoming increasingly clear. For instance, Koshima and Katsyama are existing more and more for research purposes while Takasaki, Arashiyama, and Zigokudani are developing as places of tourist attraction and for social education. The opinion now gaining popularity among Japanese scientists is that no more fresh cases of provisioning should be carried out.

In 1961 and 1962, Takeshita (1964) conducted a nationwide census of monkeys and a study of the distribution of monkeys in Japan based on findings obtained through questionnaires and on-the-spot investigations conducted from one end of the country to the other. On the basis of the study, he estimated that monkey troops numbered 425 in Japan and that the overall population stood somewhere between 22,000 and 34,000. Because there have been no censuses taken since then, it is impossible for us to discuss whether the overall population has increased or decreased from that year. But a similar investigation carried out by the Game Department in 1953 indicated that there are 313 troops, for an overall population of 15,614 monkeys in Japan. Takeshita's estimates are significant as an indicator of the effect of a ban placed on monkey hunting in 1947 by the Japanese Ministry of Agriculture and Forestry. The hunting ban has since become less rigid. The regulations have been so revised that prefectural governors are empowered to issue special hunting permits where crop damage by monkeys has gone "beyond control." In other words, it has become easier to capture Japanese monkeys than before. And this obviously is having some impact on the monkey population in Japan.

Since around 1960, complaints have increased in various parts of Japan that wild monkeys are causing a great deal of crop damage. Studies indicate, however, that because of indiscriminate felling of trees in their natural habitat, these monkeys have in most cases been forced to come down from the mountains in search of food and turn up in the fringe hamlets, villages, and towns. In Japan today, environmental disruption is reaching a critical level, and demands are being made that there must be a sweeping reappraisal of basic policies for the protection of nature. Time seems ripe that, within that context, the question of protection for monkeys be taken up. On Mount Takasaki, I am sure that the population will continue to increase and an ecological equilibrium will be maintained at least in the foreseeable future. I am also sure that the case history of Mount Takasaki monkeys may provide indications of how far we should go in protecting monkeys and what steps might profitably be taken in developing an overall plan for the protection of monkeys throughout Japan..

REFERENCES

Carpenter, C. R. (1942a). Sexual behavior of free-ranging rhesus monkeys (*Macaca mulatta*). I: Specimens, procedures, and behavioral characteristics of estrus. *Journal of Comparative Psychology* 33:113–142.

———— (1942b). Sexual behavior of free-ranging rhesus monkeys (*Macaca mulatta*). II: Periodicity of estrus, homosexual, autoerotic, and noncomformist behavior. *Journal of Comparative Psychology* 33:143–162.

Furuya, Y. (1968). On the fission of troops of Japanese monkeys. I: Five fissions and social changes between 1955 and 1966 in the Gagyusan troop. *Primates* 9:323–350.

———— (1969). On the fission of troops of Japanese monkeys. II: General view of troop fission of Japanese monkeys. *Primates* 10:47–69.

Itani, J. (1954). Japanese monkeys at Takasakiyama. In K. Imanishi (Ed.). *Nihon-Dobutsuki*, Vol. 2. Tokyo: Kobunsha.

———— (1958). On the acquisition and propagation of new food habits in the natural group of the Japanese monkeys at Takasakiyama. *Primates* 1(2):84–98.

———— (1972). The social structure of primates. In S. Morishita et al. (Eds.), *Ecology*, Vol. 2. Tokyo: Kyoritsu-Shuppan.

Itani, J., et al. (1963). The social construction of a natural troop of Japanese monkeys at Takasakiyama. *Primates*, 4(3):1–42.

Itani, J., Ikeda, J., and Tanaka, T. (Eds.) (1964). *Wild Japanese monkeys at Takasakiyama.* Tokyo: Keiso-Shobo.

Itani, J., and Mizuhara, H. (1958). Notes on malformed individuals found in the wild group of Japanese macaques at Takaskiyama. *Bulletin of Experimental Animals* 4.

Kano, K. (1964). The second fission of the natural troop of Japanese monkeys at Takasakiyama. In J. Itani, J. Ikeda, and T. Tanaka (Eds.), *Wild Japanese monkeys at Takasakiyama.* Tokyo: Keiso-Shobo.

Kawanaka, K. (in press). The inter-troop relationship of wild Japanese monkeys. *Primates* **14**(1).

Koyama, N. (1970). Changes in dominance rank and division of the wild Japanese monkey troop at Arashiyama. *Primates* **11**(4):335–390.

Masui, K., Osawa, H., Nishimura, A., and Sugiyama, Y. (in preparation). Population census on Japanese monkeys at Takasakiyama.

Mizuhara, H. (1964–1970). Free-ranging Japanese monkeys and their ecological management. *Yaen* **18–32**.

――― (1971). *History of Takasakiyama monkeys*. Osaka: Sogensha.

Mizuhara, H., Hayama, S., and Kaji, M. (1962). Report on the health condition of wild Japanese monkeys at Takasakiyama. *Yaen* **11**:3–8.

Mori, A. (1972). On the sign behaviors observed in the grooming relation of Japanese monkeys. *Annual Record of the Primate Research Institute of Kyoto University* **2**:82–86.

Nishida, T. (1966). A sociological study of solitary male monkeys. *Primates* **7**:141–204.

Norikoshi, K. (1972). On the transfer of male Japanese monkeys recorded during five years after the fission of Arashiyama troop. Paper presented at 16th Annual Conference on Primate Research, Japanese Monkey Center at Inuyama, Japan.

Sugiyama, Y. (1960). On the division of a natural troop of Japanese monkeys at Takasakiyama. *Primates* **2**:109–148.

Takeshita, H. (1964). Distribution and population of wild Japanese monkeys. *Yaen* **19–21**.

Toyoshima, A. (1968). On the third fission of a Japanese monkey group at Takasakiyama. *Proceedings of the VIIIth international congress of anthropological and ethnological sciences*, Vol. 3.

Yoshiba, K. (1965). An analysis on the human injury by monkeys at Takasakiyama Park. *Yaen* **23–24**.

Yoshihiro, S., Tokida, H., and Hara, S. (1971). On the input and output of male Japanese monkeys, a case of Shiga Troop A. Paper delivered at 25th Annual Conference on Anthropology and Ethnology in Japan, at Tokyo, Japan.

CHAPTER 11

Orville A. Smith

PRODUCTION OF SPECIALIZED LABORATORY PRIMATES WITH CONSIDERATION FOR PRIMATE CONSERVATION*

THE NEED FOR QUALITATIVELY DIFFERENT LABORATORY PRIMATES

Since its beginning six years ago, the Primate Field Station of the Regional Primate Research Center at the University of Washington, located at Medical Lake, Washington, has made progress toward the establishment of a large, stable colony of pedigreed primates of known ages for use by the local and regional scientific research community. The number of research projects supported by the facility has grown steadily during the succeeding years and the demand for animals has continuously slightly exceeded the growing ability to supply them. Within the last year, all the renovated space that could be used for housing animals has been filled.

In considering an expansion of the colony from its present size of

* This work is supported by NIH Grant RR00166 from the U.S. Public Health Service to the Regional Primate Research Center at the University of Washington.

1000 animals on four floors to 3000 animals on nine floors of the Medical
Lake facility, an evaluation was made of the needs of the scientific community. Simple production of primate infants satisfies some of the needs.
But, for the future, a more controlled and defined experimental subject
is required for many of the research programs if they are to generate
meaningful answers to complex biological problems. Development of
such a large colony must simultaneously confront the problems of conservation of nonhuman primates in the wild. The basic breeding stock
must be imported from native environments, and therefore the influence
of trapping large numbers of animals on the existence of the species
must be considered. With these facts in mind, we have considered the
approaches that would satisfy both the need for expansion to a controlled, defined colony and the major concern for conservation of the
nonhuman primate.

The goal of an expanded colony is to make available to the scientific
community a colony of primates which would provide the capability of
carrying out research across the full range of biology with sufficient
numbers of animals to make such research efficient and meaningful. This
means providing a colony of animals ranging in age from the moment
of fertilization to senescence and having these animals characterized as
completely as possible with regard to as many biological factors as possible. These factors would include parentage, growth, blood chemistries,
enzyme variants, environmental histories, and other relevant variables.
Besides the obvious use of such a colony in studying perinatal problems,
this kind of colony would also make possible the study of aging in primates and associated disorders such as senility, cancer, and arthritic and
osteological problems. The colony would provide a new means for studying the multifactored chronic diseases such as hypertension and atherosclerosis from all relevant views, including genetics, diet, psychological
and environmental factors, and aging. The colony would further provide
a foundation for future studies in genetics which would include not only
the development of special groups of monkeys, such as those with high
or low cholesterol levels, hypertension, metabolic defects, and so forth,
but also the capability of studying behavioral genetics—an urgent need
that is critical to study at the primate level.

A colony such as this would of course be available to the general
scientific community and it would provide that community with the
capability of doing research with primates at the next higher level of
sophistication and complexity, that of complete genetic, developmental,
and environmental control.

THE UNIQUE PHYSICAL FACILITY FOR PRODUCTION OF THREE CATEGORIES OF PRIMATES

The physical facilities for implementing this expansion to a specialized colony already exist at the Primate Field Station at Medical Lake, Washington. As stated earlier, the Field Station currently supports a colony of 1000 animals, primarily *Macaca nemestrina* (Figure 1), with smaller numbers of *Macaca fascicularis*, *Macaca fuscata*, and *Papio anubis*. The building, originally designed and used as a maximum security prison, has three stories with four wings perpendicular to a central core (Figure 2). Three large wings are available for animal housing and an isolated basement area serves as a quarantine. Each of the 20 animal rooms per wing floor measures approximately 2.2 × 3.4 × 2.8 meters. Each floor also has two rooms at the end of each corridor measuring 3.4 × 7.8 meters. Several of the animal rooms are equipped with multiple stainless steel cages, suspended on racks and separated from each other by acrylic panels, which were specifically designed for single-pair breeding.

This physical organization allows for various configurations of housing and breeding. Presently, three floors of one wing and one floor of another wing have been renovated and are housing animals. The numerous small

Figure 1. Adult male and juvenile *Macaca nemestrina* (pig-tailed macaque). This species is used for breeding because of several desirable characteristics: external signs of ovulation, tractability, strong maternal behavior, and size of infants.

Figure 2.   Primate Field Station at Medical Lake, Washington, a converted maximum
security prison for the criminally insane, now used for primate breeding.

animal rooms are used for harem breeding of one male with 6–8 female
monkeys and also for housing infant and juvenile animals in groups of
10–20. The large end rooms are used for breeding and housing sex-
mixed groups of 15–20 adult animals. The individual cages are used for
timed-pregnancy breeding and for holding animals with special problems.

These three types of housing allow for production of three different
categories of primates. In the harem situation, the parentage of offspring
is known and can be controlled. This makes possible the category of
mass-produced, genetically known animals. In the large mixed groups,
only the dam parentage is specifically known, but production of infants
qua infants is high with minimal manipulation and great efficiency. In
the cage situation, one male is allowed access to one female for 24–48
hours; therefore the category of accurately timed pregnancies can be
produced from specified parents.

These methods of breeding pose special problems, mainly in the area of behavioral compatibility and disease transmission, but the physical organization has already proved efficient for a colony of 1000 and seems ideal for a large colony of 3000 primates. The alternative of total individual cage housing and breeding is financially prohibitive. The opposite alternative of free-ranging compound housing is economical, but does not offer the control over matings that is necessary to produce special subcolonies of genetically manipulated animals. A combination of approaches to housing, using the harem housing as the principal type, has allowed us to satisfy the majority of needs of the biomedical research community with a reasonable degree of economic modesty.

EVALUATION OF THE CONSERVATION PROBLEM AND CONTRIBUTIONS TO ITS SOLUTION

To expand the present Field Station colony and to realize the goal of a self-perpetuating colony of 3000 animals, a large number of primates, mainly *M. nemestrina*, will have to be imported from natural sources. We presently estimate 1000 animals would initially be needed for the Primate Field Station plus a small number per year until the colony infants mature to reproductive age. This need for a supply of primates from the wild until the colony reaches the self-regenerative stage must be evaluated and activated with a concern for conservation of the species.

Macaca nemestrina are indigenous to the Malay Peninsula, Thailand, Borneo, and Sumatra. Their density in these areas is not known, but Southwick and Cadigan (1972) indicate that the species is rare in the Malaysian peninsula. All *M. nemestrina* imported to our Primate Center during the 1960s came from Malaysia. In 1970, contacts were established in Indonesia and necessary government support was obtained to permit exportation of several hundred *M. nemestrina* to the Regional Primate Research Center at the University of Washington.

Since little information existed on the abundance and distribution of this and other primate species in Indonesia, a proposal was written and submitted to the Primate Centers Program of the NIH to survey the primate population on the island of Sumatra. In October of 1971, Carolyn C. Wilson and Wendell L. Wilson began a 1½-year primate census study of the island (Figure 3). To date, they have completed and reported (1972) their findings in the three southern provinces of Sumatra— Lampung, Sumatra Selatan, and Benkulu. They have determined the relationships among the presence of each of the six species of monkey found in these provinces, the habitat type, and the altitude. In 365 hours

Figure 3.   Dr. Carolyn Wilson and Dr. Wendell Wilson on primate census survey in Sumatra, Indonesia. The infant siamang, obtained from a local villager after its mother was shot, was raised for several months and then given to the World Wildlife Fund Orangutan Rehabilitation Station at Loeser in Aceh for return to its jungle habitat.

of observation in eight locations covering an area of 35.9 square miles, they have found that *Presbytis cristata* and *M. fascicularis* are the most abundant, *Presbytis melalophos* and *M. nemestrina* are the next most abundant, and *Hylobates syndactylus* and *Hylobates agilis* are the least common. *Macaca nemestrina* have been observed in secondary lowland forest (under 1500 feet) and in primary and secondary hill forest (1500 to 3000 feet), but seem to favor the primary hill forest. They seem to be rare in terms of numbers of groups, and all those seen, except during roadside counts, were in the vicinity of farms. It appears that each group has a large home range in which it migrates, raiding farms in its "circuit." In some areas, farmers actively trap the pig-tailed macaque, since this monkey does great damage to crops. More extensive surveys of hill forests away from settled areas will be done to determine whether the densities for *M. nemestrina* are influenced by the presence of farmland. There is some evidence that in the deep forest where humans rarely go, there are relatively few animals. It may be that a certain level of human habitation is beneficial to the nonhuman primate population.

The Wilsons' field census of Sumatra will not be complete until 1973. They have surveyed one half of the island, and are now doing the north central and northern areas. From their preliminary data, however, some facts can be used to determine where and how primates should be obtained for export without it being detrimental to the existing population and, more important, how this information can be employed to guarantee the survival of the native population.

It is a reasonable assumption that farming and logging are two major factors leading to decimation of primates, the first by farmers having to protect their crops by killing marauding monkeys, the second by destruction of the natural habitats and dwelling places. These seem to be self-evident factors that need no scientific verification. However, if the observation that practically no primates are found in the deep forests and most are found on the periphery of human developments is substantiated, then the assumption needs to be examined by analyzing sound field data. To assess the importance of these factors, we have recently requested maps of logging concession areas and of transmigrant relocation areas on the island of Sumatra. With this information, "before and after" studies can be planned to evaluate the impact of these factors. We also hope to utilize this concession and transmigrant relocation information to decide where to trap the 1000 animals needed for the Medical Lake colony expansion—the thought being that animals would be captured that would otherwise starve or be killed as a result of these activities.

The information on densities and habitat may also increase the effectiveness of the Indonesian Directorate of Forestry in their management of the 27 nature reserves already established and may lead to suggestions for the establishment of additional reserves. Furthermore, a program might be initiated whereby monkeys are trapped in an area that will be needed for economic purposes and transported to another area that could support an increased primate population. Once the basic information is obtained, a whole series of recommendations should be forthcoming, some of which should be reasonable and feasible. A major contribution to conservation will be that after the large colony is established at Medical Lake, it will be self-perpetuating and further trapping from native habitat will be minimal.

The assistance to achieve some of the goals of this project may come from unexpected sources. A chance bit of information about the Weyerhaeuser (forest products) Company having an operation in Indonesia led to a visit to their home office a few miles outside of Seattle. We held very profitable discussions with their man in charge of Indonesian affairs and their Manager of Communications. The company has a large logging concession in Kalimantan (southeastern Borneo), which they plan to operate as a permanent station. They are building a complete city to provide for the 1200 workers. Their concession includes many thousands of acres of completely untraveled and unoccupied primary forest. This forest area is surveyed for timber types and sizes by teams dropped in and retrieved from these remote areas by helicopter. Initial discussions were begun with the Weyerhaeuser people about the possibility of taking the Wilsons on some of the deep penetrations to do primate surveys in this otherwise inaccessible terrain. This may be the only way that the question of numbers of primates in the remote forest areas can be obtained. This situation would also provide the perfect experimental situation to determine the impact of logging on primate populations. It could be critical to determining the influence of the *kind* of logging operation on these populations. For instance, the selective logging approach contemplated by Weyerhaeuser could conceivably lead to increased primate population by thinning the heavy forest and removing the dense canopy, thereby increasing the growth of food-bearing trees. Ground cover and small tree growth is almost nonexistent in primary forest due to the continual blockage of sunlight by the matted canopy of high branches. This selective logging operation could be assessed against the effects of clear-cut logging often carried out by other logging companies. Clear-cutting operations are obviously destructive to habitat and terrain.

PROPOSED RESEARCH STATION FOR EDUCATIONAL
AND CONSERVATION PURPOSES

The final phase in this plan is the establishment of a research station in Indonesia, probably in Kalimantan on the east coast of Borneo. This station is needed for two reasons. First, it would facilitate the gathering of detailed information on the behavior of the various kinds of primates so that scientifically based conservation programs can be developed. The history of uninformed man "messing" with his environment with honest good intent as well as with inadvertent callous indifference is filled with examples of egregious error leading to ecological disasters. A complete, informed conservation effort can be achieved only by knowing the details of group structures, social behavior, home ranges, symbiotic relationships, predator relationships, and many other factors obtainable only by carefully planned, formal field studies.

Second, if a sizable research station populated by scientists of various kinds could be established there, this would provide concrete evidence to the Indonesian government of the importance of their wildlife and would in several ways provide mechanisms to influence conservation policies in the country.

This notion of establishing a research station in Kalimantan is not without design. Such a station would need (1) to be as close to the objects of study as possible, (2) to have a base of operation that has good supply channels and transportation already developed, (3) to maintain a critical mass of scientists to satisfy the needs for intellectual stimulation among themselves, and (4) to have as broad a scientific base as possible to give the operation strength from all fields of biology—from anthropology to virology.

An east coast location in Kalimantan could eventually meet these requirements well. Within a 1000-mile radius of this point (Figure 4), one of the largest selections and varieties of the world's biology can be found. This includes the whole of Borneo; the Philippines to the north; the Malay peninsula and Sumatra to the west; Java, Bali, Timor to the south; and the Celebes, Moluccas, and New Guinea to the east. This radius would cross Wallace's line, bringing the whole of the Australian biota into reach. A well-equipped research station in this location could be used by an extremely wide range of scientists as a home base of operation.

Thinking specifically of primatology, this location would bring the orang-utan, gibbon, *M. nemestrina*, *M. fascicularis*, proboscis, several varieties of *Presbytis*, and some prosimians immediately into the field laboratory, and, within only a short distance, the siamang and the Celebes ape.

If such a plan as this is to be realized, it would have to incorporate two additional major objectives: (1) involvement of Indonesian scientists to the fullest extent possible, and (2) provision of an educational facility to train Indonesian students in biology so that they may some day be the leading scientists in the biology of their own country. Too frequently scientists do field work in a foreign country without regard to the potential benefit to the host government if information, techniques, and training

Figure 4. The 1000-mile-radius area around Kalimantan, proposed location of a research station, containing one of the largest selections and varieties of the world's biology.

were shared. In the case of a permanent field station, ignoring these objectives of involvement and training would not only mean ultimate failure of the project, but also would constitute an immoral act on the part of those involved.

SUMMARY OF PLAN FOR PRIMATE PRODUCTION AND CONSERVATION

A future requirement by the scientific community for the production of highly specialized primates has been identified. A permanent, stable colony of 3000 *M. nemestrina* will be required to make a beginning toward meeting that need and to ensure the capability of the colony being self-perpetuating. A facility at Medical Lake, Washington, has been developed as a unique site for such a colony. In this facility, three major needs of the biomedical community can be met with minimal costs, that is, mass production of infant monkeys, high-volume production of genetically known monkeys, and production of precisely timed fetuses. A colony numbering 1000 animals is already functioning toward these ends.

A proposal has been submitted to increase the colony to the required 3000. Simultaneously, a plan has been initiated to provide for the conservation of *M. nemestrina*, as well as other indigenous primate species, in Indonesia. This involves, first, a census of all primates on the island of Sumatra, which is over half completed; next, it involves gathering data on logging and farming developments that influence natural wildlife habitats. These data will be used to determine areas where *M. nemestrina* should be trapped for shipment to Medical Lake rather than allowing them to be destroyed by these commercial programs. The information will also be transmitted to the Indonesian Department of Conservation to aid them in their planning for effective primate conservation procedures.

The final facet of the overall plan involves the establishment of an Indonesia-based field station which would be used to further research relevant to conservation of many Indonesian primates. It would also contribute scientific information to the total field of biology.

Figure 5 is a summary flow chart of scientific requirements, facilities available and needed, actions designed to achieve the goals, and ultimate relevance to conservation of the primate population.

ADDENDUM

The paper was written and presented to the conference about eight months ago. Since that time the following progress has been made toward achieving the stated goals.

1. A grant request for the partial expansion of the Primate Field Station at Medical Lake, Washington, has been approved but awaits funding.

2. The Wilsons have completed the survey of Sumatra.

3. A map of planned and already operational logging areas on Sumatra has been obtained. The map also shows transmigrant relocation areas, both government sponsored and spontaneous (individual initiative).

138

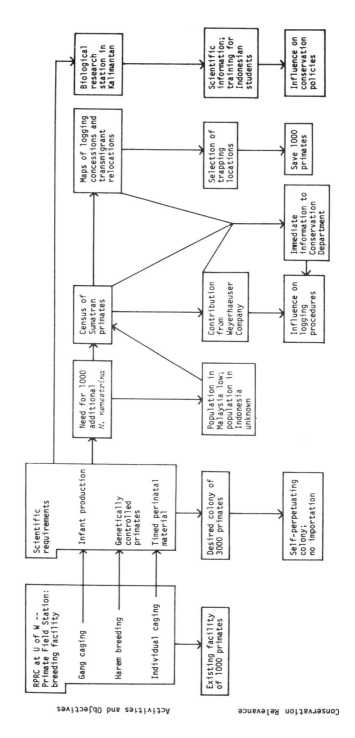

Figure 5. Flow chart of the activities, facilities, and objectives in the plan for conservation and production of specialized laboratory primates.

4. A cooperative study with the Weyerhaeuser Company has been initiated. The Wilsons are at the Weyerhaeuser logging operation near Balikpapan, East Kalimantan. They have already done a survey of primate densities in a selectively logged area compared with an undisturbed area of primary forest. The study of primate density in climax forest is in progress.

5. A meeting to plan for a research facility in Borneo was held in Seattle. The planning group included Donald Lindburg, David Horr, Peter Rodman, Dorothy Reese, and the author.

6. Through finances provided by the School of Medicine, University of Washington, a small field research facility has been established in the Kutai Nature Reserve on the east coast of Kalimantan, a cooperative venture with the Indonesian Directorate of Forestry and Nature Conservation Office. The land for the station and matching monies were provided by the Indonesian government. The station consists of two multiple-unit buildings and some equipment. Donald Lindburg and Nick Fittinghoff are currently using the facility for a study of *M. fascicularis.*

ACKNOWLEDGMENTS

Ideas and words pertinent to this plan have been contributed by many individuals including Dr. Erich S. Luschei, Dr. Gerald A. Blakley, Dr. William R. Morton, Dr. Carolyn C. Wilson and Dr. Wendell L. Wilson, and Ms. Dorothy Reese, who also helped write this paper.

REFERENCES

Southwick, C. H., and Cadigan, F. L., Jr. (1972). Population studies of Malaysian primates. *Primates* 13:1–18.

Wilson, W. L., and Wilson, C. C. (1972). *Preliminary Report: Census of Sumatran Primates.* On file with Lembaga Ilmu Pengetahuan Indonesia, the Indonesian Institute of Sciences, and with the Regional Primate Research Center at the University of Washington.

CHAPTER 12

Anita Schwaier

TUPAIAS–LOW-COST PRIMATES FOR MEDICAL RESEARCH

Tupaias, as you know, are considered to be "doubtful primates." Although debates on their relationship to this order are still going on, there is generally little doubt that these animals resemble primitive primates more closely than they do insectivores and that they are related to the precursors of the primate order.

You will probably ask why we became so interested in this odd species. The first reason is that tupaias can be bred in large numbers within a short time. This can be done in usual laboratory animal rooms and with low cost. Tupaias are small, can be held in one hand, and do not hurt when biting. Breeding with high success rates is possible if present knowledge of their behavior is considered. The second reason is of special significance in Germany: there is neither an alternative breeding program nor a primate center where primates are made available for research. Strict quarantine rules related to imported animals cause additional problems. The third reason is that the metabolism of tupaias can be assumed to have a greater similarity to that of man than that of dogs or rats or other nonprimates. The numerous anatomical analogies that led to the classification of tupaias as primates will almost certainly be reflected in similarities in their physiology.

This assumption of a higher degree of metabolic correspondence with primates was recently supported by Williams (1971) of St. Mary's Hospital Medical School in London, who found that in the case of the metabolism of sulfadimethoxine, tupaias react like primates. Other experiments on fat metabolism (Chaffee et al., 1968) and the effect of cyproheptadine (Opitz et al., 1971) gave similar results.

For these reasons we feel that in all cases in which rodents are unsuitable as animal models, it would be reasonable to look at the tupaias before taking into consideration dogs or even monkeys. The financial risk would be much lower than with monkeys and dogs.

OUR EXPERIENCE WITH BREEDING TUPAIAS

A prior condition for successful use of tupaias in research is, of course, a thriving breeding colony that yields uniform animals in large numbers. Moreover, the animals must be fairly easy to handle. Although we are just beginning this type of breeding program, our preliminary results are quite promising.

To establish a breeding colony of tupaias, we had to distinguish among various subspecies offered by the animal dealers. In Germany, tupaias are usually imported from Bangkok, but it is impossible to learn the exact place where they were trapped. There are about 50 species or subspecies of tupaia and nobody seems to be able to distinguish among them. In the literature, tupaias from Bangkok or its vicinity are called *T. glis*, *T. chinensis*, or *T. belangeri*, and in one case *T. tana*. For this reason, it would be most useful to establish criteria for their differentiation. One criterion to distinguish animals of the *T. glis* group from those of the *T. chinensis* group is the number of nipples, first reported by Lyon (1913). The animals of the *T. glis* group, which are normally obtained from Kuala Lumpur, have two pairs of nipples, whereas the animals of the *T. chinensis* group have three pairs. Moreover, it was shown by Arrighi (1969) that the two groups have different numbers of chromosomes. *Tupaia glis* from Kuala Lumpur has 60 chromosomes and *Tupaia chinensis* from Bangkok has 62. Our animals have three pairs of nipples, and in the first chromosome preparation of one of our animals 62 chromosomes were found—analogous to the counts in *T. chinensis* by Arrighi.

Bangkok seems to be a region where at least two subspecies integrate. This would explain the large variation in the size of the animals, which has also been noted by Chaffee (1969). The weight of his animals, which he called *T. chinensis*, ranged from 120 to 250 grams, similar to that of our animals. In Germany, Martin (1968) and von Holst (1969), who had been in Bangkok, classified their animals as *Tupaia belangeri*, whereas this subspecies belongs to the *T. chinensis* group in the classification of Lyon (1913). Their animals correspond to the larger animals of our colony. Because we will select only the larger animals for future breeding, we decided to call our line *Tupaia belangeri* (chinensis group). Our measurements of head and body, tail, and skull for this group are in good agreement with those of Lyon.

A peculiar problem in breeding tupaias is their special sensitivity to stress. Only pairs with fast pair bonding, which do not fight, will breed at regular intervals of 45 days. The animal under immediate stress can be recognized by the ruffling of tail hairs (von Holst, 1969) and after prolonged stress by weight loss, underdeveloped scent-marker glands, and in males by decreased size of the testes and their retracted position.

In our Frankfurt laboratory, the following provisions were made to reduce the environmental stress: The breeding pairs are kept in a quiet room at the end of our building, with room temperature of $24 \pm 3°$ C, humidity at about 50 percent, and automatic lighting for 12 hours. The animal keeper is advised to spend as little time as possible in the breeding room, especially on days when births are expected. A standard pellet diet with 24 percent protein was developed and has proved to be very satisfactory.

For rapid cleaning, we have sheets of corrugated paper underneath the cages that can be exchanged quickly. Our cages are covered with a curtain of dark fabric. Tupaias seem to like a dark background, which gives them a feeling of security. The animals are not allowed to see their neighbors, which is essential to avoid social stress. There is no agreement about the minimum space required for one pair. Morris et al. (1967), who also explored breeding requirements of captive tree shrews in Bangkok, recommended much smaller cages than we are using, but had high abortion rates. Martin and von Holst in Germany proposed cages several times larger than ours for high breeding success. The size of our cages, ½ cubic meter, seems sufficient, but we feel that the tubes connected to our cages (see Figure 1), which allow the animals to retreat, are very important. The tubes are of plastic and easy to clean, and animals can be extracted from them with ease.

Every pair can be watched unseen, which is necessary for ascertaining whether the couple is in balance or not. If fighting occurs, the partners must be separated and exchanged. If a female accepts a newly introduced male, copulation will occur immediately. The females are fertilized repeatedly also during pregnancy until a few days before term.

In our Frankfurt laboratory, we have one room of medium size and an adjacent small one where we keep 17 cages with 17 pairs we selected

Figure 1. Tupaia breeding cage, with nest box and sleeping box outside the cage.

from 22 males and 28 females. In January 1972, two months after introduction of our standard diet, several births occurred. Subsequently, we
had about 20 young born every month and an average of 9 young reaching weaning age every month. In Table 1, you can follow the breeding
success in our colony during the first six months. In January, seven
females had their first litter, and in June, five had their fourth litter. In
our colony, we now know the cycle of every female, and even if we
could not improve the survival rate of 50 percent, a colony of this size

Table 1   Sequence of Births in the First Six Months of 1972

Number of Litters, Young, and Survivors	Jan.	Feb.	March	April	May	June	Total
First litters	7	4	2			1	14
Second litters	2	3	5	4	1		15
Third litters			3	1	4	4	12
Fourth litters	1			1	2	5	9
Fifth litters			1			2	3
Sixth litters				1			1
Seventh litters						1	1
Total litters	10	7	11	7	7	13	55
Total young	23	18	24	15	17	26	123
Total survivors at weaning	8	11	8	9	13	13	62 (50%)

would yield 10–15 animals per month. Theoretically a production of 300 animals could be achieved per year.

Females are fertile for at least three years. In Table 2, the intervals in days between births for each female with more than one litter are noted. There are admirable regular breeders, such as female B, and others that always breed irregularly. Births may occur at different times of the day or night. It has been assumed that postpartum heat lasts for only 2 hours. We will soon be able to decide whether this is true.

Some peculiarities of female breeding behavior should be mentioned, which were first described by Martin (1968), but were not generally believed. Newborn tupaias have very large stomachs (Figure 2). They can drink an amount of milk equaling nearly half their body weight. The mother visits the nest only every 48 hours, which results in a rising and falling weight curve with an increase every other day. Martin stated that tupaia milk consists of 25 percent fat. This is an extreme value, which has been verified by our chemists. Hand-rearing is therefore very difficult. All our experiments with different milk compositions failed or resulted in extremely meager animals with disturbed behavior.

Von Holst (1969) found a clear relation between the extent of stress and breeding performance in female tupaias. Stress was measured by the time interval during which the tail appeared ruffled. With increasing stress periods, first the feeding rhythm will be disturbed and milk production will be diminished, then the litter will be eaten after birth, at stress times about 20–44 percent owing to the lack of scent-marking

Table 2 *Intervals in Days between Births*[a]

Litter							Female								
	A	B	C	D	E	F	FA	G	J	M	N	O	P	R	U
1	42	44	45	41	45	44	*54*	43	*120*	43	41	43	*52*	*64*	45
2	41	44	44		45	40	42	45	*54*	43	43	44	44	44	*96*
3	42	42			44	42		*52*	*53*		*62*	42	45	42	
4	43	42										43			
5		44													
6		42													

[a] Normal: 40–45 days (80%) (exceptions to this norm are in italics); average: 43.1 days.

Figure 2. Two young *Tupaia belangeri*, 1 hour after birth.

behavior. The females will then become sterile, lose weight, and finally die if the stress time lasts longer than 90 percent of the daytime. In our colony, cannibalism is rare, but the regular feeding rhythm of 48 hours is sometimes disrupted. In those cases, females feed every day, but smaller amounts of milk are consumed in total.

The most frequent number of young per litter is two (Table 3). Litters of three are reduced by us if the female is small. We also had one litter

Table 3   Litter Size in Tupaia Belangeri

Number of Young per Litter		Number of Litters
1		3
2		38
3		14
4		1
Average: 2.23	Total:	56

Table 4   Weights of Young Tupaias (in grams)

Sex	At Birth			At Weaning (one month after birth)		
	Maximum	Minimum	Average	Maximum	Minimum	Average
Male	19.3	9.1	12.9	135	77	106
Female	20.0	9.1	13.4	139	71	105

of four animals, which was reduced to two. The ratio between newborn males and females was 55 males to 63 females.

Table 4 shows the large differences in the weights of newborn tupaias. The differences are mainly due to the different milk amounts in the babies' stomachs. Well-suckled babies have doubled their body weight after 6 days and have four times their body-weight after 12 days, such as the one shown in Figure 3. The young tupaias are mature at 4–6 months of age (Figure 4). Our youngest mother had her first litter at an age of 5 months.

Figure 3.   Twelve-day-old baby of *Tupaia belangeri*.

Figure 4.   An adult male *Tupaia belangeri*.

The high rate of regular births gives us the possibility to establish timed embryological stages of tupaias. One female was killed 12 days after copulation. She had three implantations, which were at the 13-somite stage. Therefore, a delay of implantation of about 20 days, as postulated by Martin, can no longer be assumed.

THE POTENTIAL FOR TUPAIAS IN RESEARCH

After we have coped with the breeding problems, we will undertake experiments to investigate the usefulness of tupaias as an animal model. Our program includes basic information on hematology and clinical chemistry, teratology, and diabetes research. In the literature, spontaneously occurring diabetes in tree shrews is reported. We are trying to induce diabetes in some of our tupaias by a diet rich in calories. The pancreas in tupaias is more compact than in rats and may be well suited for *in vitro* experiments.

Another potential application for tupaias is infarct research. Rats, for instance, are not sensitive to the effects of glycosides, and tupaias might be better models for that area. Also, tupaias may be particularly useful because stress has such a distinct effect on this species.

Further experiments are planned in the fields of tumor induction, inhalation toxicology, and toxicology of fertility-regulating agents.

It may thus be concluded that tupaias are promising experimental animals for future research in many fields, regardless of their low position in primate phylogeny.

REFERENCES

Arrighi, F. E., Sorenson, M. W., and Shirley, L. R. (1969). Chromosomes of the tree shrews (Tupaiidae). *Cytogenetics* **8**:199.

Chaffee, R. R. J., Sorenson, M. W., and Conaway, C. H. (1968). A study on chemical thermogenesis and chemical thermosuppression in the "protoprimate" *Tupaia chinensis*. *XXIVth International Congress of Physiological Sciences*, Washington, D.C.: Federation of American Societies for Experimental Biology.

Holst, D. von. (1969). "Sozialer Stress" bei Tupaias (*Tupaia belangeri*), *Zeitschrift fuer Vergleichende Physiologie* **63**:1–58.

Lyon, M. W. (1913). Tree shrews: an account of the mammalian family Tupaiidae. *Proceedings of the United States National Museum* **45**:1–188.

Martin, R. D. (1968). Reproduction and ontogeny in the tree shrews (*Tupaia belangeri*), with reference to their general behavior and taxonomic relationships. *Zeitschrift fuer Tierpsychologie* **25**:409–495, 505–532.

Opitz, K., Weischer, M. L., and Klose, L. (1971). Der Einfluss von Cyproheptadin auf die Nahrungsaufnahme in Tierversuch. *Arzneimittelforschung* **21**:957–961.

Williams, R. T. (1971). The metabolism of certain drugs and food chemicals in man. *Annals of the New York Academy of Sciences* **179**:141–154.

CHAPTER 13

Keith R. Hobbs

THE FEASIBILITY OF SUPPLYING RELATIVELY LARGE NUMBERS OF PRIMATES FOR RESEARCH

INTRODUCTION

This paper is concerned with the feasibility of supplying relatively large numbers of primates to the research community, especially in the United Kingdom, although the ideas could apply to other countries. The reasons for considering the production of primates in the countries of origin and the likely costs compared with those in the user country (the United Kingdom) will be discussed. These costs are based on theoretical estimates and, to a limited extent, practical experience.

I would like to thank Professor Annie B. Elliott, of Nanyang and Singapore Universities, and Dr. Louis S. B. Leakey,* of the Tigoni Research Centre near Nairobi, who gave a great deal of time and thought to various proposals, and the detailed costing and estimates that I discuss are a direct result of their work. I must stress that although these figures, the subject of careful consideration, are not based on practical experience of large-scale free-range breeding of primates, they do reflect the local costs and conditions of maintaining laboratory animals and buildings.

* Dr. Louis Leakey died in October 1972.

CURRENT USE AND SUPPLY

The use of imported wild-trapped primates in research has long been an anomaly. On the one hand, research workers have emphasized the need for high-quality laboratory animals (and, indeed, conventionally bred and hysterectomy-derived stock of laboratory rodents and lagomorphs is commonplace today). On the other hand, there has been no attempt to breed primates for general supply, even though the literature is full of references to the hazards of using these animals when obtained from their natural environment. It is recognized that there are many establishments throughout the world where various species of primates are successfully bred, but these colonies usually exist only to supply animals for the organization that breeds them. The number of animals produced in the laboratory does not have any significant effect on the overall numbers of primates needed for research. Only 2.5 percent of all primates used in the United Kingdom are bred in the laboratory, which represents approximately 250 animals every year. In the United States, the equivalent figure is 5 percent, or approximately 3500 animals every year (ILARS, 1968, 1970, 1971).

Approximately 94 percent of all primate work in England is being carried out on seven species of monkeys and 85 percent of this on only four species. While recognizing that certain specialized species may have to be bred, it appears that not enough emphasis has been placed on breeding those species most commonly used. This is further reinforced by the October 1971 report of the U.S. Institute of Laboratory Animal Resources which lists 62 species of primates being maintained in 711 laboratories throughout the United States. No less than 33 of these species are being bred in varying numbers, although 80 percent of all primate work in the United States is carried out on only five species.

Of the 9000 primates used in the United Kingdom every year, approximately half are used for acute studies such as vaccine production and testing. The remaining half are used in about 20 other fields of study, usually of a nonacute nature. The task of breeding for both these categories would be formidable, and it would be unrealistic, at least to begin with, to consider breeding programs on this scale. While recognizing the benefit of using bred primates for vaccine work, there are those who feel that breeding for this purpose would be impracticable and uneconomic. Certainly in the United Kingdom, the organizations involved in vaccine work already have very efficient systems of screening imported animals and it is debatable whether breeding for this purpose is justified.

It is also possible that to try to satisfy too large a demand at first might prejudice the concept of breeding primates for any type of work.

However, there is no doubt that the provision of bred animals for use in the nonacute studies involving approximately 4500 primates per year is more than justified and it is the investigators in these fields who would derive the most benefit. It must be stressed that we are not only talking about the need to produce numbers of primates as a source of supply, but also the need to provide research workers with the means to undertake research that at present cannot be done without primate breeding programs. Examples of these studies include immunology (especially fetal and neonatal), genetics, growth, development and aging, teratology, fertility, antifertility, and nutrition in infants and pregnant animals.

There is little doubt that supply creates demand. This has already been shown in the use of conventionally bred and specified-pathogen-free (SPF) laboratory rodents and lagomorphs. The important factor is that the supply should be reliable and sufficiently large to respond to present research demands. If, for example, 1000 primates were produced annually in the United Kingdom, they would represent approximately 25 percent of those used in work other than vaccine preparation.

In the United Kingdom, the Medical Research Council Laboratory Animals Centre administers an Accreditation Scheme for the large-scale production of the commonly used species of laboratory animals (Bleby, 1967). This means that commercial breeders produce animals under the direct quality control of the Medical Research Council, which provides expert advice both to the research user and the supplier. There is no reason why laboratory primates should not also be eventually provided through this system, although it would take several years to produce the number of animals suggested and it would be very expensive initially in the United Kingdom. It is felt, therefore, that the idea of establishing breeding programs overseas, at least for an interim period, should be investigated because:

1. The problem of supply exists now and a large number of animals could be produced in a relatively short time.

2. Capital costs and current expenditure would be less, since land, buildings, labor, and maintenance are considerably cheaper than in the United Kingdom.

3. Various problems of large-scale colonies could be more easily and cheaply investigated than in the United Kingdom.

4. Meanwhile, the knowledge gained overseas could be used in the

breeding programs in the United Kingdom, where research workers would probably have come to expect the use of a bred animal and would pay appropriate prices.

It would be desirable for the user country to be responsible for overseas breeding schemes so that it had control of the management, quality, and supply of animals, and a very close working liaison with the research workers receiving the animals.

It is recognized that the animals would still have to be imported and undergo some form of quarantine. But because in the United Kingdom imported primates are obliged by law to be quarantined for six months in approved premises* (where research work can be carried out during this period), establishments using these animals will already have suitable accommodations. The advantage is that they will receive animals of known history and higher quality than hitherto.

COSTS

Primates bred for research work have usually been produced by the research establishment requiring them and the cost has, understandably, been very high because a research institute has to support expensive equipment and buildings and is not the place to breed primates most economically. Consequently, quotations for laboratory-bred monkeys are usually exorbitant, and as there are no commercial units breeding primates for general supply there are no reliable figures on which to base costs.

Theoretical Costs

A formula that has proved reliable in producing estimates for breeding other laboratory species, and to which I referred at the Berne meeting in 1971 (Hobbs, 1972), was used in a theoretical costing experiment for the commonly used primates. It showed that:

1. For macaques, assuming a reproduction rate of one offspring per female per year, production costs would be in the region of $190† per

---

* Under the Rabies (Importation of Mammals) Order, 1971, made under the United Kingdom Government Diseases of Animals Act, 1950.
† All dollar amounts given in this paper are in United States dollars.

animal, but if the reproduction rate dropped to 0.6 offspring per year (the average in the wild), the figure would be $315. If it can be assumed that under optimal conditions in captivity an intermediate figure applied, the cost would be about $260.

2. *For marmosets*, the estimate would be $85. The cost for this species is substantially less because it is sexually mature at 17 months and will produce an average of three young per year. It is also much smaller and thus more economical to house than macaques.

3. *For squirrel monkeys*, although they are also smaller than macaques, the average reproduction rate is only one offspring per year and, therefore, the cost would be in the region of $170.

It is stressed that these figures are based on 1971 costs and *do not* include profit margins which a commercial undertaking would have to consider. These theoretical costings were compared with figures obtained from commercial concerns in the United Kingdom and based on practical experience in breeding primates within their own concerns.

Practical Costs

The examples given below are the only serious attempts so far to cost commercial breeding programs in the United Kingdom and are based on actual experience and would apply to programs producing at least 100 animals per year:

1. Two leading pharmaceutical companies considered that it would cost $470 to produce a three-year-old macaque. If supplied at, say, one year of age, the cost would be approximately $225.

2. Only one commercial concern was able to give reliable figures for marmosets. These were based on maintaining offspring to at least six months of age, when they would cost $90 each.

It is interesting that the theoretical costing exercise follows very closely the figures produced by the practical costings. This suggests that for the purpose of breeding and maintenance, there is no reason why laboratory primates cannot be regarded in the same way as other commonly used laboratory animals which are specifically bred for research. It is from these commonly used species that the costing formula has been derived.

The figures represent a two- to threefold increase in the present price of a quarantined primate from the wild. (This disparity will almost certainly lessen as the wild animal becomes scarcer and its price rises.) As it is almost certain that the purchase price of the research animal represents less than 10 percent of the total cost of a project, the overall increase in expense of using bred primates will be small, but the validity of the experiment will be increased and the other advantages arising from its use will be great.

As experience in the large-scale breeding of primates increases, it is more than likely that costs will be reduced, since there will be savings in overhead costs and continual improvements in breeding techniques.

Cost of Overseas Breeding Establishments

The only estimates obtained from overseas that deserve serious consideration have come from Singapore and Nairobi and, as mentioned earlier, they are the work of Annie B. Elliott (Elliott, 1972) and Louis Leakey, respectively. They present different approaches to the problem, although they both have emphasized that labor, land, building, and maintenance costs are cheap compared with those in the United Kingdom. They also have emphasized that the responsible authorities (in the case of Singapore, supported by the government) are anxious to cooperate with recognized organizations and that land is already available on established academic sites.

Nairobi. The work of the National Primate Centre at Tigoni is well recognized and at least 11 species of African monkeys have already been successfully bred there. Leakey stressed the need to start any large-scale breeding schemes with a pilot project, suggesting the use of vervet monkeys with 300 animals housed in a ratio of 1 male to 5 females. He pointed out that no accurate cost for a bred monkey can be given until a three-year trial period has been undertaken. If the trials are successful, he suggested that the schemes be passed to a government or private concern and not remain the responsibility of the National Primate Centre at Tigoni.

Preliminary estimates of the costs of such a scheme are given in Table 1. The table does not reflect the costs that most organizations would have to consider, because land and some maintenance staff would be provided by the National Primate Centre. It also does not take into account the cost of academic staff that may be employed either from the user country or from the Tigoni Centre.

Table 1   Tigoni Proposed Cost Estimates

Capital items	Cost (U.S. $, converted from £)
50 outdoor cages	1,700
Site preparation for cages	560
Transport	5,400
Capital equipment	250
Procurement of 300 vervets	6,750
Total	14,660
Maintenance items—first year	
Salary for manager	1,500
Subsidized rent for manager	950
Other salaries and contingencies	1,400
Food for 300 monkeys	4,000
Vehicle maintenance, petrol, insurance, etc.	1,400
Total	9,250

It is estimated that by the end of the second year the first batch of bred monkeys would be ready for sale. Although Leakey did not suggest a production cost for an animal, his estimates indicate that it would be most unlikely for a four- to six-month-old vervet monkey bred within his scheme to exceed $68.

Singapore.   Anne B. Elliott of Singapore goes into rather more detail and suggests a larger scale of operation. In her estimates (which are based on 1970 costs), she considers breeding macaques and derives her information from the experience of workers in Nanyang and Singapore Universities in housing and breeding large numbers of laboratory animals and in housing and occasionally breeding small numbers of macaques.
The following information has been used in Elliot's calculations:

1. Land is cheap, from $0.30 to $3 per square foot.
2. Development costs are from $2000 to $3000 per acre.
3. Building costs range from $1.20 per square foot for the *cheapest* possible permanent building, that is, with honeycomb brick wall, wooden frames, wire mesh, and open drainage channels, and rendered mosquito proof, to $4 per square foot for buildings of orthodox brick wall, controlled ventilation, covered drainage, and rendered mosquito proof.
4. Caging would range, according to quality, from $50 to $80 for approximately 300 cubic feet to house 10 adult monkeys or *pro-rata* family groups.

5. Food would cost approximately $0.50 per day per animal for a pelleted diet containing 22 percent protein supplemented with fruit and nuts. Facilities would be available for local preparation of any required monkey chow.

6. At least $24,000 per year should be allowed for adequate staffing of the enterprise.

7. Young adult macaques would cost approximately $30 each, unconditioned.

No allowance has been made for the cost of conditioning the initial stock or for subsequent routine screening of the colony, including offspring. A rough estimate to include these would add approximately 5 percent to the cost of each young adult produced.

Certain assumptions have to be made, as follows:

- Harem conditions are used with six females to every one male per cage (approximately 300 cubic feet).
- Males and females reach maturity at four years.
- Females should be progressively depleted during a reproductive span of six years.
- For the purposes of costing food and accommodation, it would be assumed that two young monkeys are equivalent to one adult.
- All surplus young adults of both sexes are taken to be usable products from the breeding colony.
- For every single young adult monkey produced per year, the colony must provide food and housing during that year for the equivalent of two adult monkeys.
- Each female of reproductive age, after allowing for wastage, is calculated to produce one offspring per year.

Development of the Colony. It is suggested that *1000 young adults should be produced per year.* To do this, the site and buildings would be progressively developed over a period of four years and the employment of staff increased. The young adult stock and the few youngsters resulting from breeding will be accumulated over this period.

All expenses for the first four years would total $210,000. If this is regarded as a capital investment, it must bear interest at, say, 10 percent per annum. To allow for this, $21,000 must be charged against all future years and in addition the annual recurrent expenses would total $45,000. Therefore, the production costs for 1000 young adult monkeys per year

Table 2   Cost of Scheme to Breed 1000 Macaques Annually in Singapore[a]

	Capital Expenditures (U.S. $)	Annual Recurrent Expenditures (U.S. $)
Year 1	$51,000	$ 18,200
Year 2	16,300	27,500
Year 3	7,000	45,000
Year 4	Nil	45,000
Total costs over first four years		$210,000

[a] Estimates provided by Annie Elliott and Lim Kok Ann, Nanyang University, Singapore.

would be $66,000, giving a cost per monkey of $66. A summary of the initial investment for the first four years is shown in Table 2.

Elliott acknowledges that various unforeseen factors might delay or diminish production and that it might well be five or six years before production reached target figures. It must be realized that no allowance has been made in these figures for the cost of exporting animals to the user country (the United Kingdom). At an estimate of $5 per kilogram body weight for freight charges, an additional 10 percent could be added to Elliott's figures.

Another omission is an allowance for the salaries of skilled staff from the user country which, calculated at about $15,000 per annum, would entail an increase of approximately 20 percent on the cost of each animal. As a result, it may be more realistic to say that the cost of such a scheme, producing 1000 young adult macaques per year at a usable weight of, say, 1½ kilograms each, would be in the region of $80 per animal when it lands in the importing country, and probably $100 by the time it is ready for use. This is still less than the current price of the *conditioned* wild-trapped animal about which nothing is known and which, even after undergoing a period of quarantining and medication, is usually still diseased.

Summary of Proposed Development Plan. It seems that the Singapore proposal is the most attractive and its advantages may be summarized as follows:

1. The site is offered at a nominal rate and is part of an established university of high academic standing. There is a comprehensive range of graduate staffing whose expertise would be available for the scheme. The Singapore government is extremely keen to participate with respon-

sible research organizations and would encourage the use of the university facilities.

2. The social conditions of Singapore are good and are certainly comparable with Western European and American standards.

3. The availability of skilled personnel is good and the standard of training is high and comparable with that of the West.

4. The up-to-date airport is on main international routes and offers excellent facilities.

The disadvantages must also be recognized. The cheaper type of outdoor accommodation used for breeding would entail difficulties in controlling insect- and avian-borne diseases. On the other hand if more expensive type of enclosed building with controlled ventilation were used abroad, it would still be considerably cheaper than similar accommodation in the United Kingdom. The animals would still have to undergo the stress of export by jet, although transport arrangements and conditions are likely to be more easily controlled by a national organization, as it would have more authority in dealing with airlines than the average exporter.

SUMMARY

The proposals discussed above could be the start of a large-scale production of primates under controlled conditions, and the advantages of an overseas station for breeding primates far outweigh the disadvantages. An overseas breeding station would provide:

1. large numbers of primates that could be produced relatively quickly and at minimal cost;

2. a realistic quantity and a reliable supply of bred primates;

3. nearly 25 percent of the present United Kingdom market for bred primates;

4. supplies that would almost certainly create an increasing demand, making the concept of breeding laboratory primates in the user country a reality; and

5. knowledge which woud be gained at minimal cost prior to establishing similar programs in the user country.

As it is almost certain that conservation demands will enforce breeding of research primates in the next few years, the sooner such projects are undertaken the better. Lastly, it must be emphasized once again that further detailed investigations must be undertaken before considering the proposed cost estimates quoted in this paper.

ADDENDUM*

The British Medical Research Council is currently considering the cost proposals as part of a report submitted as a result of a survey carried out by the author into the current use, supply, and future provision of nonhuman primates for biomedical research in the United Kingdom. It is hoped that the report will be published once the Council has made its deliberations known.

REFERENCES

Bleby, J. (1967). The function and work of the United Kingdom Laboratory Animals Centre. *Laboratory Animal Care* **17**(2):147–154.

Elliott, Annie B. (1972). Estimated cost of breeding macaques in Singapore. (Paper delivered at W.H.O. International Symposium on Breeding Nonhuman Primates for Laboratory Use, Berne, Switzerland, June 1971.) In W. I. B. Beveridge (Ed.), *Breeding primates*. Basel: Karger, pp. 111–113.

Hobbs, K. R. (1972). Breeding simians for U.K. research needs. (Paper delivered at W.H.O. International Symposium on Breeding Nonhuman Primates for Laboratory Use, Berne, Switzerland, June 1971.) In W. I. B. Beveridge (Ed.), *Breeding Primates*, Basel: Karger, pp. 174–179.

Institute of Laboratory Animal Resources (1968, 1970, 1971). *ILAR News*, Vols. 12(1), 14(1), 15(1), respectively.

* Just prior to submission for publication, this postscript was added by the author to apprise the reader of current progress made on this effort.

CHAPTER 14

Robert A. Whitney, Jr.

A DOMESTIC PRIMATE PRODUCTION FEASIBILITY STUDY

Domestic sources of supply of nonhuman primates for biomedical research have long been recognized as an essential area for development in the United States. Over 65,000 primates are used annually in United States research laboratories and 60 percent of these animals are rhesus monkeys (*Macaca mulatta*).

Many factors have discouraged private enterprise from initiating large-scale production of rhesus monkeys. Investors are dissuaded by the initial high cost of quality breeding stock and facilities for domestic production and the length of time between initiation of the breeding colony and production of significant numbers of salable offspring. It is also a significant factor that imported, wild-trapped, rhesus monkeys are readily available today at prices much lower than costs estimated for those produced by even the most efficient domestic breeding methods.

Given the current availability and cost of feral rhesus monkeys, there are still many compelling reasons for immediate development of domestic supply. The wild-trapped primate used in research today is a very-poor-quality research animal. Usually, the age, origin, disease background, and environmental history of these monkeys are totally unknown. They may be carriers of diseases infectious to man and hazardous to other nonhuman primates. Another important factor is the consistent depletion of the species in the wild. It is obvious that there is not a limitless supply of wild primates. Some are already in the endangered species category. Although this is not yet the case with the rhesus monkey, destruction of habitat, killing as pests by local residents, and long-term trapping for export are taking a toll of the wild rhesus populations.

Although these factors present a clear case for developing a significant domestic supply of primates for research, an additional special circumstance demonstrated the severity of the situation: an international political crisis. In 1971, during the height of the India–Pakistan war, commercial traffic was prohibited from Indian airports. This resulted in a complete halt of exportation of rhesus monkeys for a short period. The impact of the sudden, complete cessation of supply prompted the Animal Resources Branch, Division of Research Services, National Institutes of Health (NIH), to initiate promotion of domestic production of rhesus monkeys.

THE NEED FOR A DOMESTIC PRODUCTION PROJECT

The need for demonstrating the feasibility of a domestic semifree-ranging primate breeding operation was felt by NIH to be essential to the eventual production of research animals in sufficient numbers at a realistic and reasonable cost. A small number of rhesus monkeys were already being bred in NIH-supported Primate Research Centers throughout the United States and in small numbers at several universities and commercial laboratories. These monkeys represented less than 3 percent of the total number of rhesus used in United States biomedical research and, in almost all cases, the young were being used for intrauterine or neonatal research work. The costs for young from these breeding programs varied from $400 to $700 each at birth.

Clearly, the existing programs of individual cage breeding and gang cage or harem breeding could not produce numbers to significantly supplement or replace the more than 700 rhesus imported into this country every week. In fact, these breeding programs were in no way meeting the current demand for timed-pregnant and neonate rhesus monkeys.

In early 1972, the Animal Resources Branch (ARB), Division of Research Resources, NIH, began development of a cost-sharing contract for a rhesus production project. The "Request for Proposals" (RFP), as advertised in the *Commerce Business Daily*, described the purpose of the project as follows: "To design, promote, and assist in evaluating the commercial feasibility for domestic production of free-ranging rhesus monkeys in a restricted area."

The scope of work in the contract basically required the contractor to:

1. provide the breeding colony stock at his own expense (with all breeders and progeny the property of the contractor);

2. provide the required physical facilities and environment necessary to maintain free-ranging monkeys in a restricted and protected area, as well as proper quarantine facilities;

3. provide specific testing and treatment procedures to define all animals prior to their release from quarantine and introduction into the breeding colony environment;

4. convene, in cooperation with ARB, a panel of experts in the field for guidance in developing the project;

5. develop and evaluate a variety of techniques and facilities essential to the operation, such as monitoring techniques, shelter devices, feeding systems, watering devices, and capture systems;

6. develop a screening program for diseases and monitoring of physiological values, reproduction data, and behavioral patterns and problems;

7. provide a complete analysis of costs, determine the scale of operation required for commercial success, and define the animals produced in this operation; and

8. determine the feasibility of raising a well-defined, healthy, rhesus monkey from a free-ranging breeding colony at a cost favorable to the supplier and to the user.

The specific aims of the Division of Research Resources were to produce information that could be made available to the general public and to promote the quality of the operation by sponsoring expert guidance. It also would enhance long-term development of the breeding operation by sharing costs of the expensive, early stage of growth of the operation which yields no income to the contractor.

THE CHARLES RIVER BREEDING PROJECT

Four formal responses were received to the RFP. An *ad hoc* expert committee evaluated these proposals and selected the proposal submitted by the Charles River Breeding Laboratory in Wilmington, Massachusetts. This company has been a leader in breeding animals for many years. The Charles River proposal committed a 90-acre island in the Florida Keys for this project. The island, Key Lois (formerly known as Loggerhead Key), is 1.9 miles from the nearest key, but is relatively convenient to major transportation facilities. It is only 3 miles from U.S. Highway 1.

After conducting a nationwide survey of the existing domestic supply of rhesus monkeys, it was determined that capture of wild rhesus monkeys for initially setting up the breeding colony was the only feasible approach. Special precautions were taken in trapping and holding these monkeys.

Under the surveillance of a veterinary epidemiologist well qualified in primate husbandry and disease control, a special expedition was organized. Monkeys were trapped in an area in India as remote to human population as possible, examined for herpetic lesions, tuberculin tested, and measles vaccinated in the field. Trappers wore face masks and gloves. Special shipping/holding cases were constructed, drinking water was boiled and then chlorinated, and baked biscuits were specially prepared as food for the captured monkeys.

The monkeys were moved from trapping areas in the shipping/holding crates to an isolated holding area at New Delhi Airport in trucks disinfected with phenolic detergent. The monkeys were not subsequently transferred from these containers, but remained in the same crate from the time of initial capture until removed at the quarantine facility. Special advance shipping arrangements were made with the airlines to minimize the waiting time in Delhi. No other nonhuman primates were transported with these monkeys or were subsequently placed aboard the aircraft. The international flight was met by the contractor with fumigated, air-conditioned trucks for final transport to the quarantine compound at the Charles River facility in Massachusetts.

ADDENDUM*

Initial progress has been excellent. An additional group of 180 rhesus monkeys trapped in March 1973 are also in quarantine in the Wilmington facilities. There have been no positive tuberculin reactors, no diarrhea, and no deaths in the group of monkeys. The initial group of monkeys have been immunized against measles, tetanus, and rabies, and have been tested for B-virus, tuberculosis, shigella, and salmonella. Positive animals have been eliminated, and all remaining monkeys are negative to these tests. The canine teeth on the large males have been clipped. They have also been wormed and a multiple virus profile is being compiled.

---

* Just prior to submission for publication, this postscript was added by the author to apprise the reader of current progress made on this project.

An extensive ecological survey of the island has revealed almost no vertebrate life except migratory birds and one species of lizard. There was no evidence of any mammalian life forms on the island. A dock and corral with feeders and waterers has been constructed on Key Lois and a base facility on Summerland Key adjacent to Route 1 has been purchased to use as a staging area and laboratory facility. The initial group of 67 breeders was introduced onto Key Lois in June 1973. Since then an additional 550 breeders have been added. Over 16 infants have been born on the island since June 1973, and the anticipated breeding population will be 1200–1300.

CHAPTER 15

Donald G. Lindburg
Gordon Bermant

SUMMARY: PRIMATE UTILIZATION AND CONSERVATION

Phylogenetic closeness to man provides the rationale for utilization of nonhuman primates in biomedical research. The advantage to be realized from study of these near relatives is that they frequently offer the closest analog or homolog to the human condition of medical concern. The monkey or ape becomes a stand-in for the human, allowing experiments that could not be performed directly on people. The unique qualifications of a number of primate species for particular investigations have been demonstrated repeatedly in recent years (Muchmore and Davis, 1971). However, there are also many examples of unnecessary and wasteful biomedical use of nonhuman primates. In the face of dwindling natural supply and inadequate domestic breeding resources, it seems a wise course of action to scrutinize every use of monkeys and apes to determine whether sound and rigorous criteria for legitimate exploitation have been met.

It has been pointed out repeatedly that more than 90 percent of the primates used in academic and industrial research in the United States and United Kingdom are harvested from naturally occurring populations (see Chapters 2 and 13). The modest needs of other user countries are met almost entirely through import of wild-trapped subjects.

While it is practically impossible to determine with precision the number of primates required domestically on an annual basis, recent surveys by the Institute of Laboratory Animal Resources (ILAR) provide reasonable estimates, as well as information on the species most in demand. The ILAR reports are based on questionnaires that have been sent to known and probable users each year since 1966. The rate of response to these questionnaires has ranged from approximately 50 to 70 percent, which in reality accounts for a higher percentage of the actual number of primates used, since the major users are among the respondents (Thorington, personal communication).

The decline in number of primates imported into the United States since the peak year of 1968, as shown by the ILAR figures, is attributed to reduced levels of federal support for research and to more efficient utilization of imported subjects (see Chapter 2). Decline in number of animals used by the pharmaceutical industry parallels the overall trend toward reduced numbers of imports (Chapter 4).

Current use patterns indicate that the rhesus monkey, *Macaca mulatta*, accounts for about 50 percent of all primates used in research. However, several New World species are being used with increasing frequency; the major factor leading to the increased use of at least one neotropical primate, *Aotus trivirgatus*, is its remarkable suitability for study of specific human disease problems.

Predicting future needs on the basis of recent uses and trends is as fraught with risk as any technological projection. Growth in primate facilities and in number of investigators employing primate models suggests that further decline in total annual consumption is unlikely. The possibility of an opposite trend is one factor cited as grounds for establishing domestic breeding facilities. New information on model suitability (Chapter 3) and bans on export of wild-caught subjects by supplier countries (Chapter 14) are examples of events that defy prediction and that may affect future use of particular species. These factors, coupled to the rate at which the habitats of currently available species are being destroyed, provide a compelling incentive for the development of alternatives to reliance on the wild-caught primate.

PRESENT RESOURCES

Several chapters in this volume and other recent publications (e.g., Beveridge, 1972) indicate the scope of current efforts toward providing domestically reared primates as an alternative to feral imports. Although these efforts are impressive, it is unlikely that the current reliance on imports will be appreciably diminished in the near future. Even a slight rise in total annual needs would more than offset the numerical gains achieved through current levels of domestic production.

Arguments for the desirability of large-scale domestic breeding programs are so conclusive that little advantage would seem to be gained by further examination. Moreover, it seems to us that there is sufficient technical knowledge to carry out breeding programs on at least some species at the appropriate scale. The difficult questions seem to be in setting priorities for the scope and nature of different potential programs and the species to be used in them. Many of the relevant factors involved in these decisions have been discussed throughout the chapters presented here. In our opinion, nevertheless, there is no consensus among the experts, except perhaps to proceed as vigorously as possible on as many fronts as possible and await developments. In the presence of ever-tighter budgets in all but a few fields (e.g., cancer research), this view provides little help to the policy maker.

When one changes the focus of concern from utilization to conservation of currently available resources, one discerns that the demographic data base from which plans and programs might be constructed is, typically, inadequate. The notable exceptions are *(1)* the periodic surveys of *Macaca mulatta* in north India by Southwick and colleagues (Chapter 5), *(2)* the recently concluded survey of Sumatra by a team from the Washington Regional Primate Research Center (Chapter 11), and *(3)* the multifaceted investigations of the primates of Colombia and Peru which are under way at the present time (Chapter 6). Apart from these efforts, information is virtually nonexistent that would indicate priorities in species to be selected for breeding or that would establish the level of harvesting for export that a given species can support.

The information collected by Cooper and Hernandez-Camacho (Chapter 6) could serve as a model for future activity. Their report of species' distribution and abundance, economics of the primate trade, varied forms of exploitation, government attitudes, legal restrictions on export, conservation efforts, and so on, gives a total picture for a major exporting country that is probably unequaled. Even though a number of their findings are of a preliminary nature, they provide a basis for deciding where future efforts should be concentrated. It is recognized that these kinds of data may be more difficult to acquire in some countries than in others, and in fact they may be so costly in terms of manpower and time that the worth of the effort might be questioned. More modest field surveys are unquestionably a substantial bargain for both conservation and research interests, however. For the research community there is often an additional payoff in the form of information that can be used to improve colony management.

From field reports it is clearly evident that habitat destruction poses a major threat to a number of primate species (Chapters 6–8). On the other hand, there are indications that some species thrive in secondary forest and may therefore benefit from some degree of habitat disturbance. Given these possibilities, provision for resurvey at no more than five-year intervals should be built into the future picture as a means of monitoring population trends.

NEW CONCEPTS IN PRIMATE PRODUCTION

Validity of research findings when wild-caught primates are used is a source of worry to many investigators, since the animals are of unknown quality. Disease history is one of a number of background parameters that affects subject quality; in some investigations this information is critical. Other commonly desired kinds of information are precise age, parentage, reproductive history, and early social environment. Since these data are relatively easily acquired in the controlled captive environment, domestic-reared subjects are regarded as superior to those imported from the wild. Enhanced quality is thus an added incentive to establishment of domestic breeding facilities.*

In designing domestic breeding facilities, the importance attached to such factors as cost, available space, convenience in maintenance, and species-specific needs will determine whether a more or less free-ranging colony or, at the other extreme, individual caging is most suitable. All the alternatives permit the collection of data on disease and reproductive and developmental histories as well as on precise age and female parentage. Where exact knowledge of paternity or conception time are important, then only harem, pair, or individual caging permits the necessary environmental control. The cost of producing animals under these varied systems may be expected to vary in direct proportion to the amount of human control exerted over the production process.

---

* However, it would be erroneous to assume that the colony-raised primate is uniformly superior or essentially equivalent to the wild-caught animal. Research regarding functions that are highly susceptible to influence by neonatal environmental factors (e.g., neuroendocrine functions, behavior) ought to account for possible differences in experimental outcomes based on these factors. This point is raised again below.

It is yet to be determined whether the most cheaply produced domestic product can compete economically with wild-caught animals when the investigator has a choice. Obviously, future needs can best be served if a forced choice between "high-quality but expensive" and "low-quality but cheap" animals can be avoided. With the possible exception of animals that fulfill special requirements such as timed pregnancies, or those species that will breed only under very special conditions, the best solution is a breeding system that can achieve high productivity while at the same time maintaining low unit cost and satisfying the largest number of user requirements.

The semifree-ranging colony with either natural or artificial barriers to movement would seem to offer great promise for most of the species now in demand, provided disease problems can be adequately controlled.* The Cayo Santiago colony of *Macaca mulatta* has proven the reproductive potential of island facilities (Carpenter, 1972) even though breeding has not been its main objective. To the management practices already established on Santiago could be added such procedures as deliberate alteration of adult sex ratios (reduction in number of males), culling out of aged, injured, malformed, diseased, and nonproductive members, annual or biannual trapping for harvesting of "surplus" juveniles, and so on. At least five of the nine species listed by Goodwin (Chapter 2) as most in demand could probably be managed in this fashion.

A variant on the island colony approach is one in which restraint on animal movement is imposed by providing necessary food at only a small number of locations. As used by Japanese workers in behavioral studies with a number of species, most notably *Macaca fuscata* (Chapter 10), this approach entails use of the management procedures outlined above, with colonies that are maintained in relatively small areas of forest used by the animals for resting, social activities, and supplemental feeding. The Takasakiyama (Chapter 10) *Macaca fuscata* have maintained generally good health over many years despite high animal density and high frequency of contact with humans. On the negative side are the losses of animals either through migration or unexplained disappearance, but these could probably be controlled by limiting group size. "Ranching" schemes of this nature are most feasible in resource country locations.

---

* Reproductive histories under these conditions are limited, of course, to such readily observable events as age of sexual maturation, mating behavior, and pregnancies. In those instances where more detailed information is desired, there is no alternative but to use more restrictive and costly facilities.

Another example of an approach that holds promise of producing quality primates at reasonable cost is the plan discussed by Hobbs (Chapter 13) for a breeding compound based in Singapore. Although more elaborate in facility design than is the case with free-ranging colonies, its overseas location allows for development and operation at a lower cost than would be possible in major user countries.

There are two principal arguments advanced against resource country facilities: (1) political instability of resource country governments, and (2) lack of control over colony management procedures that would insure high-quality animals. Certainly the first of these objections has not deterred private enterprise in other areas from exporting capital and expertise and importing a useful product, nor should the risk of investment be considered uniform for all resource countries. The second objection is the more serious one. It is puzzling, however, that there should be a reluctance on the part of user countries to provide personnel and training for overseas operations. The increased costs that would be incurred would be confined to the initial years of operation and can therefore be used as an argument against such commitments only if one takes the short-term view. Involving resource countries more directly in rational exploitation of their own natural resources is surely desirable on moral grounds as well (see also Smith, Chapter 11). Success of these programs would require the commitment of resources that are available primarily to those national authorities concerned with domestic-based breeding schemes.

The research community's position as a "consumer" of a valued natural resource requires that it give attention to the relationship between research needs and conservation efforts. Despite a continuing lack of definitive information, there remains no reasonable doubt that survival of a number of primate species is endangered. It is further evident that no species is presently threatened as a consequence of exploitation for biomedical programs (Southwick et al., Chapter 5; Harrisson, Chapter 9; and Harrisson, 1971). Decimation of habitats by lumbering and farming interests and utilization of primates for food or pelts are recognized as the major threats to species survival. Nevertheless, we believe all users have an obligation to lend their special knowledge of primates to the solution of conservation problems. This might take a variety of forms, such as providing advice to governments or educating colleagues on practices that might reduce import levels (Cadigan and Lim, Chapter 8). Contacts with businesses involved in habitat modification, such as the Washington Regional Primate Research Center's interaction with major timber interests (Smith, Chapter 11), can be productive in gaining access to remote areas for population surveys and could eventually lead to opportunities for study of the effects of logging on certain populations. Additionally, of course, such contacts can heighten the conservation-consciousness of the commercial interests. Field surveys, such as the Sumatran survey (Chapter 11), which take an area approach and yield information on species of value both to research and conservation interests, deserve added support from the user community. While it is true, as Harrisson (Chapter 9) points out, that most user-sponsored studies reflect special interests, the foregoing examples illustrate programs that yield data relevant to the user's legitimate research activities as well as information on species of no immediate research interest.

RECOMMENDATIONS FOR FUTURE ACTION

The following recommendations for action are a distillation of views expressed during conference discussions and in follow-up letters circulated by the conference organizers to participants. They are not to be regarded as formally adopted positions, but rather as points of concern that were raised in the interest of improving communication and generating further discussion or action.

Maximum Utilization of Available Resources

The number of individual primates required for research may be reduced through maximum use of fewer animals. By this approach, a researcher needing stock for a project would seek discards or surplus animals from other users before turning to feral subjects. Assuming that animals can be located whose prior use does not disqualify them, the researcher who takes this course not only aids in conservation, but enjoys some advantage in acquiring subjects with fewer unknown characteristics than newly conditioned imports. He may also realize an economic advantage if his only acquisition cost is payment of shipping between laboratories. This kind of exchange program is already in operation; additional organization is required to make it maximally effective.

Another useful aspect of animal recycling would be to make available to other users organs or parts from animals used in acute studies. Once needs of this nature are satisfied, remaining materials would be channeled to educational and research institutions for use in instruction or for building skeletal collections. Numerous institutions exist that would pay shipping costs for whole or partial cadavers if they had access to information on when and where such materials could be obtained (see, for example, Mittermeier and Fleagle, 1973). Consignment of primate cadavers to the incinerator following sacrifice for the eyes or kidneys is an extremely wasteful, though regrettably common, practice. We are rapidly approaching the point where practices of this nature can no longer be condoned, given the continued heavy dependence on wild primates to satisfy user needs.

Success of these programs requires the development of adequate channels of communication between users. One immediate result of the Battelle Conference was agreement by the Primate Information Center of Seattle, Washington, to publish notices of primate needs and surplus animals in its *Current Primate References*. The *Laboratory Primate Newsletter* is another publication that regularly carries notices of this nature on a quarterly basis. Use of these services is purely voluntary, and after a suitable time period users should be contacted in order to assess effectiveness. It seems likely that matching needs with resources on anything more than a voluntary basis will require an extended effort in compiling and disseminating information. In all major user countries, national authorities exist that could function as a centralized clearing house for such programs, but they will need to develop some means of acquiring on a regular basis more complete data than is currently available.*

Other suggestions that would have a conserving effect require granting agencies to take a more active role in regulating animal use. For example, agencies might require the grantee to:

- state the rationale for his choice of subjects.
- use "approved" stock whenever available, and assist him in locating same.
- report surplus animals that may become available during the term of his grant, and develop plans for disposal of subjects upon project completion or grant termination.

The last of these suggestions leads to consideration of a "warehousing" arrangement whereby surplus animals or materials are held at a central location until required by another user. Some authorities believe a ware-

---

* Hobbs (personal communication) reports that such information is available in the United Kingdom through the Ministry of Agriculture, which licenses all quarantine facilities.

housing scheme for live animals is unworkable, however, because of the high costs and probability of serious disease problems. An alternative may be to earmark funds that could be used by grantees to maintain their surplus animals in their own premises until another user can be found.

Education of Users on Species Suitability

The criteria that are applied in selecting species for academic or industrial uses have been discussed in recent publications (e.g., Muchmore and Davis, 1971; Schmidt, 1969). Of particular concern are those choices that are made without regard to availability or species characteristics and that may therefore work to the disadvantage of either the animal or the user. For this reason it is felt that much would be gained by developing a set of guidelines to aid researchers in choosing animals for their studies. This is a necessary, but formidable, undertaking. The greatest difficulty is in the area of species differences in suitability as models for specific kinds of disease problems. Unfortunately much of the critical information, in addition to being widely scattered in the literature, is of a tentative nature and therefore subject to different interpretations. The best approach may be sponsorship of a working committee by a centralized agency in a position to provide necessary support. The committee should be international in nature, composed of representatives from a broad spectrum of the research community and from industrial users. It should include persons with knowledge of availability as well as of biological characteristics, for there is little to be gained in recommending use of species in short supply regardless of their suitability on other grounds. Guidelines so produced should be published and disseminated through every means available, possibly including governmental regulatory and funding agencies.

Support of Specific Programs in Husbandry and Breeding

It was noted in an earlier section that current breeding efforts produce considerably less than 10 percent of the annual biomedical primate requirements. In the majority of cases these programs are instigated by research institutions that desire to produce animals for their own use. An exception is the California Primate Research Center at Davis, California, which has entered into a contractual arrangement with the National Institutes of Health to produce rhesus monkeys for sale to NIH grantees. Whitney (Chapter 14) describes a second effort by NIH to contract for breeding of rhesus monkeys, in this instance with private enterprise.

More precise identification of user needs and resources than is presently available would serve as a guide to areas where additional effort should be concentrated in future breeding programs. It is indeed gratifying to note that the NIH has recently provided support for a major effort at acquiring the necessary information. A résumé of the program, published in *ILAR News* (October 1973) is reproduced here in the interest of increasing awareness of activities in this important area.

The Committee on Conservation of Nonhuman Primates was organized in March 1970 to examine the distribution and abundance of the nine most commonly used species of nonhuman primates and to assess the effect of harvesting on indigenous population levels. At present there are a number of conflicting statements—but little sound data—on the impact of exportation. The committee is conducting field studies of selected South American primates in Colombia and Peru through a subcontract with the Pan American Health Organization.

With support from the Division of Research Resources, National Institutes of Health, ILAR has employed a full-time staff officer (primatologist) familiar with techniques employed in literature reviews and field surveys. The staff officer is working under the guidance of the Committee on Conservation of Nonhuman Primates and is reviewing the existing scientific literature relative to population dynamics and extracting and assembling the data that provide a realistic picture of nonhuman primate populations in the wild.

The assembled data will later be correlated and judgment of those species in short supply that are of value to biomedical research will be made. Based on assembled information, the committee will select an appropriate area of the world for field surveys of those species considered to be the most critical for research purposes.

The final report, when assembled, should provide a current assessment of natural populations of primates on a worldwide basis by:

- Identifying those species or subspecies of nonhuman primates critical for biomedical research that are rapidly being depleted.
- Identifying possible alternative sources of supply of nonhuman primates critical for biomedical research that are rapidly being depleted.

- Identifying environmental parameters (e.g., food, habitat, behavioral characteristics) essential for maintenance of adequate primate populations, either in the wild or in breeding centers.

Support of these efforts by researchers and national authorities in other user countries would be helpful. The need is for cooperation on an international basis, for although the United States is the greatest consumer of nonhuman primates, the results to be obtained from these programs will be of great benefit to countries with more modest needs as well.

Recommendations regarding programs most appropriate to meet future needs, for example, indoor caging, breeding compounds, island or ranch operations, and so on, should be possible once these data are in hand.

In concert with breeding is the need to acquire information about relatively unknown species, with an eye toward increasing research options in the future. The prospect of additional breakthroughs in attacking human disease problems provides grounds for searching among primates for better models. This search needs to be conducted with careful regard to the current availability of the species and its capacity to adjust to a captive environment. There should also be a parallel commitment to development of basic expertise in breeding and management of the species that can be drawn upon as the occasion arises.

The Battelle-Frankfurt research laboratory has taken a slightly different approach to the problem, by developing competence in the breeding and management of a species whose research usefulness is as yet unproved (Chapter 12). Tree shrews (*Tupaia*) have had the reputation of being difficult to maintain in captivity and for this reason have received little attention as research animals. While their precise taxonomic status remains in doubt, they are in many respects closer to man than any nonprimate mammal. In addition, they are of small size, produce multiple young, and have a short generation time. Their potential suitability for many of the programs now using primates either less abundant or more costly to produce and maintain should be a high priority investigation of the near future.

In breeding for research, provision must be made for concurrent study of a variety of parameters that will affect production levels. These include disease problems, aspects of the physical environment such as spatial requirements and cage configuration, temperature and noise tolerances, diet, and behavior. Particular attention should be given to the long-term consequences of captive breeding. The colony-born primate is often easier to maintain than its feral counterpart, indicating a greater tolerance for the stressful stimuli of captivity as a result of exposure to them as infants. As yet there are very few studies directed toward acquisition of baseline data against which to measure these "adaptations" or their consequences for validity of research results.

Support of Conservation Efforts

When acted upon, a number of the foregoing recommendations will indirectly benefit the conservation effort. In-most instances the benefit will be to the least endangered species. Of more direct significance for presently threatened species is the recently launched effort by the Institute of Laboratory Animal Resources, with support from the National Institutes of Health, to compile data and initiate field surveys to determine the status of natural populations. With this information, researchers and governments can at least be advised as to optimal use patterns. Whenever possible, programs can be initiated to conserve portions of the natural habitat where endangered species are found.

It is evident that establishment and preservation of reserves must compete with agricultural and lumbering interests. It is also clear, as seen in the data provided by Cooper and Hernandez-Camacho for Colombia (Chapter 6), that it is unrealistic to expect developing countries to give the same priority to conservation as found in user countries. The task is thus a difficult one. Conservation is largely a matter of persuasion, and the appeals to conserve that have recently been adopted and published by a number of large influential organizations is an indication that efforts to increase awareness of the potential depletion of a number of species are beginning to pay off. The recent development of a preserve in Cameroon reported by Gartlan (Chapter 7) is particularly encouraging. As we have noted elsewhere (Bermant and Lindburg, 1973). we believe that the research community is in a position to take the lead in developing both conservation and production programs. This it must do if its research future with primates, and the primates themselves, are to survive.

REFERENCES

Anonymous (1973). Institute of Laboratory Animal Resources, Committee Activities. *ILAR News,* **17**(1):6–7.

Bermant, G., and Lindburg, D. G. (1973). Report on the conference "New concepts in primate production." *Journal of Medical Primatology* **2**:324–340.

Beveridge, W. I. B. (Ed.) (1972). Breeding primates. *Proceedings of the International Symposium on Breeding Non-Human Primates for Laboratory Use,* Berne, June 28–30, 1971. Basel: Karger.

Carpenter, C. R. (1972). Breeding colonies of macaques and gibbons on Santiago Island, Puerto Rico. In W. I. B. Beveridge (Ed.), *Breeding primates.* Basel: Karger, pp. 76–87.

Harrisson, B. (1971). Conservation of nonhuman primates in 1970. *Primates in medicine.* In E. I. Goldsmith and J. Moor-Jankowski (Eds.), Vol. 5. Basel: Karger.

Mittermeier, R. A., and Fleagle, J. C. (1973). A primate distribution program to end wastage of sacrificed specimens. *Laboratory Primate Newsletter,* 12(2):1–3.

Muchmore, E., and Davis, J. (1971). Biological parameters of simians for medical research. In *Proceedings, third international congress of primatology, Zurich, 1970.* Vol. 2, *Neurobiology, Immunology, Cytology,* Basel: Karger pp. 194–204.

Schmidt, L. H. (1969). Selection of species for various uses. In *Using primates in medical research, Part 1: husbandry and technology.* W. I. B. Beveridge (Ed.), Primates in medicine, Vol. 2, Basel: Karger, pp. 28–36.

Author Index

Subject Index